MW00698081

DR. GREG &
ERIN SMALLEY

Little Book *of*
Great Dates

Tyndale House Publishers, Inc.
Carol Stream, Illinois

The Little Book of Great Dates
© 2013 Focus on the Family

ISBN: 978-1-58997-772-3

A Focus on the Family book published by Tyndale House Publishers, Inc., Carol Stream, Illinois 60188.

Focus on the Family and the accompanying logo and design are federally registered trademarks of Focus on the Family, Colorado Springs, CO 80995. Date Night Challenge is a trademark of Focus on the Family.

TYNDALE and Tyndale's quill logo, and *LeatherLike,* are registered trademarks of Tyndale House Publishers, Inc.

All Scripture quotations, unless otherwise indicated, are taken from the *Holy Bible, New International Version*. NIV*. Copyright © 1973, 1978, 1984 by Biblica, Inc.™ Used by permission of Zondervan. All rights reserved worldwide (www.zondervan.com). Scripture quotations marked **NASB** are taken from the *New American Standard Bible*, Copyright © 1960, 1962, 1963, 1968, 1971, 1972, 1973, 1975, 1977, 1995 by The Lockman Foundation. Used by permission. (www.Lockman.org.)

Italicized words in Bible verses were added by the author, for emphasis.

The use of material from or references to various websites does not imply endorsement of those sites in their entirety. Availability of websites and pages is subject to change without notice.

Editorial contributors: Don Morgan, Megan Gordon, and Marianne Hering
Cover and interior design by Stephen Vosloo
Back cover photo by Luke Davis, Main Street Studio

Library of Congress Cataloging-in-Publication Data is available for this book by contacting the Library of Congress at http://www.loc.gov/help/contact-general.html.

This book was adapted from *Take the Date Night Challenge* by Greg and Erin Smalley, © 2013 Focus on the Family.

Printed in China
1   2   3   4   5   6   7   8   9   /19   18   17   16   15   14   13

Contents

Introduction

Think about some of those good times you and your spouse spent together prior to tying the knot. Can you remember the excitement? The sense of discovery? Can you recall what it felt like to learn about his or her favorite childhood memories? To talk about the experiences—both good and bad—that made each of you who you were at the time? To spend time laughing, talking, praying, and sharing your dreams, only to realize, at the end of the process, that you had fallen in love? What a magnificent experience!

"Yes, but that was then and this is now," you might be saying. "We're married! We don't need to pursue each other anymore. It's a done deal. We learned all we needed to learn about each other during the seasons of dating and engagement, and now it's full steam ahead. We're one flesh, baby! And besides, who has time to go gallivanting around town like a couple of college kids? There are more than a few other things competing for our attention at the moment, not the least of which is raising our kids to respect God, and pursuing gainful employment, and . . ."

Unfortunately, that mind-set rarely leads to a happy marriage. And if we're honest, in God's design for marriage, couples aren't supposed to take a break from emotional intimacy. You may add new titles to your lives as the years go by—"parent," "manager," "homemaker," and so on. But through it all, you still retain the titles you were given by the pastor when you were first married: husband and wife! You have added additional titles and roles as the years have passed, but you still are, and always will remain, husband and wife.

RECLAIMING COUPLE TIME

Perhaps you've had two or three kids by now. You love them more than life itself. You wouldn't trade them for anything. And yet sometimes, you look back on your years of dating, both prior to and after marriage, and you wonder what happened. You miss having "couple time"—the opportunity to relax, connect, and just focus on each other without distraction.

We know personally how difficult it is to make date nights a regular part of marriage. One time, I (Greg) was trying to get Erin out of the house for our date night. Our four-year-old daughter, Annie, didn't want Mommy to leave. She was crying and had literally wrapped her arms and legs around Erin's leg. I knew that I needed to quickly intervene, or we wouldn't be going out. But before I could say anything to Annie, our ten-year-old son, Garrison, jumped in.

"It's okay," Garrison gently spoke to Annie. "We need to let Mom and Dad go out. This is how they keep their marriage strong." Erin and I were flabbergasted. Annie released Erin and then asked Garrison, "But what do they do on their date?"

You could instantly tell that Annie had stumped him. He thought about it for a few seconds and then responded, "I'm really not sure. But I think that it ends in kissing."

That's my boy!

HARD WORK PAYS OFF

The point of the previous story is that we've worked hard to teach our kids that Mom and Dad "must" spend time together without them to keep our marriage strong.

This is not to brag. It's only to say that it's hard—*incredibly* hard, sometimes—for us to make the time necessary to invest in our husband-wife relationship, with no distractions. The professional and ministerial work of studying marriage and helping others build stronger marriages doesn't leave us much room to invest quality time in our own! Yet we make it happen. And we firmly believe you should, too!

In our counseling experiences, we've seen too many couples who try to coast through the childrearing and career years without making time to deepen and nurture their own marriages. It's a recipe for disaster.

Those couples who don't date may achieve financial stability, and they might even successfully raise their kids and navigate them through school. But they reach the empty-nest years and realize that they're strangers living under the same roof. By then, it's incredibly difficult to reverse the damage wrought by decades of essentially ignoring each other and clinging to the false assumption that they can pick up at fifty-five exactly where they left off at twenty-five.

Date Nights Done Right

We're not suggesting that simply cramming a date night into your already overcrowded schedule is going to prevent you from experiencing the unfortunate scenario we just described. But a commitment to date nights done right can definitely play a significant part in an overall plan to be *intentional* about investing in the health of your marriage.

Here are the five important dos and don'ts to keep in mind as you think about planning your dates together and endeavor to make them as fun, enjoyable, and meaningful as possible:

1. Don't administrate your marriage—
   Don't talk about finances, household responsibilities, child discipline issues, or other administrative aspects of your

marriage while on your date. The purpose of a date is to have fun and enjoy each other.

2. **Stay current** — Be curious about your spouse. Ask questions. Update your knowledge and deepen your understanding of each other.

3. **Try new and exciting activities** — Couples who engage in unique activities that they don't usually do experience an increase in marital satisfaction. New activities stimulate the same parts of the brain that were ignited when you were first dating and help recreate the chemical surges of early courtship.

4. **Reminisce** — Talking about special moments or memorable events allows you to celebrate how far you've come as a couple and renews hope as you anticipate future good times together.

5. **Select dating activities that communicate intimacy to both of you** — For men, intimacy is built on a shared activity; for women, a shared activity is a backdrop to deep conversation.

GO FORTH AND DATE

Now that you have the basics down of what makes a great date, the only thing left to do is go out and put them into practice! This little book will provide you with some very specific date ideas to take you through an entire year of dating—or more, depending on your dating frequency.

Keep in mind, this isn't the final word on marital dating. It's only a tool to motivate you and get you thinking about how to foster intimacy and connection in your marriage through regular, intentional dating. But it won't work unless you apply your own creativity and ideas to the dating process. Use your collective imaginations, but don't overthink or overcomplicate the process. As long as you're enjoying yourselves, connecting, and developing deeper intimacy, you're on the right track.

So without further ado, get ready to dive in and experience the Excitement of marital dating. It's fun, it's meaningful, and it has the potential to revolutionize your relationship! We wish you God's richest blessings as you embark on this journey together.

Now it's time to get down to brass tacks. You may appreciate knowing *why* marital dating is so important, but your primary interest is in *how* to make it happen.

You need ideas. You need inspiration. You came to the right place!

Each of the following dates will include some suggested activities as well as topics of conversation and questions for you to ask each other during the course of the date. Keep in mind that all of the activities, questions, and conversation topics are merely suggestions; they aren't hard-and-fast rules. We encourage you to think creatively and inject your own thoughts and ideas into your dates! The important thing is that your activities and discussions are consistently fun and interesting, allowing you to relax, enjoy each other's company, and connect.

Before every date, whether you're following one of the templates in this book or creating a date of your own, remember to always act as if you're trying to get a second date! Sometimes in marriage we forget that we need to pursue and woo our spouses. It doesn't matter whether you've been married for two weeks or twenty-five years, you still need to put your best foot forward when it comes to marital dating. So dress up a bit. Be polite and open doors. Compliment each other. Be affectionate, hold hands, cuddle, and steal kisses. And remember to protect your date night from conflict by cutting off any arguments and agreeing to talk about issues at a later time.

To make dating a habit—a regular event—we encourage you to commit to at least one date per month. Be sure to put your dates on the calendar so that you can schedule around them! If you're not intentional about setting aside the time, it likely won't happen. If your schedules and budget allow you to go on more than one date per month, so much the better.

1 A NEW YEAR'S DATE

The object of a new year is not that
we should have a new year. It is that
we should have a new soul.
—G. K. Chesterton

LET'S FACE IT, IN TODAY'S world the idea of New Year's resolutions is often met with a fair amount of cynicism. Resolutions were made to be broken, right? Whether it's losing weight or starting an exercise program or reading the Bible more, most people start with the best of intentions, only to discover by mid-February (if they even make it that long) that they've gotten completely off track.

But what if you could work on a resolution in partnership with someone else? That's the beauty of a marriage-related New Year's resolution! In resolving to invest in your marriage, to have a monthly date night, or to set other positive goals for your relationship, you automatically have someone in your corner who is pursuing the same goals and will encourage you in your resolution. Why? Because having a stronger marriage is something couples work on *together*. It's a resolution that can be accomplished only as a *team*.

ACTIVITY: *With the idea of new goals and new beginnings fresh in your minds, consider making this a morning date. Rather than going out for dinner, go out for breakfast and talk about setting positive goals for your marriage while you're both fresh and wide awake. If you're typically not a morning person, be sure breakfast is accompanied by lots of coffee or a similarly caffeinated beverage! If breakfast isn't your thing, think about doing another morning activity together, such as working out, playing racquetball, or going for a hike.*

 QUESTIONS: *Either during your activity or afterward, discuss the following Questions: What are some positive goals we can set for our marriage over the next six months? The next year? How can we work together to achieve these goals? Is there a specific area you feel God wants us to work on together, as a team, to make our marriage the best it can be?*

2 WE'RE A TEAM!

Coming together is a beginning,
staying together is progress, and
working together is success.
—Henry Ford

THE BEST TEAMS ARE PASSIONATE about their goals. If you're going to be part of a Super Bowl championship team, you need to do more than just wear the uniform. You need to be committed to your team's success. Individual players don't win games; *teams* win games. The same is true in marriage. Being married means doing more than just wearing a wedding ring. Rather, you wear the ring as a symbol of the commitment you made before God and humankind to be united. In every sense of the word, a husband and wife are a *team*.

The Bible reminds us that "the body is a unit, though it is made up of many parts; and though all its parts are many, they form one body. So it is with Christ" (1 Corinthians 12:12). And so it is with your marriage. Each of you brings your own personality, experiences, and viewpoints to the table, but at the end of the day, you work together as a single unit. That's the beauty of marital teamwork!

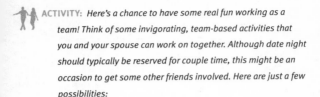 **ACTIVITY:** *Here's a chance to have some real fun working as a team! Think of some invigorating, team-based activities that you and your spouse can work on together. Although date night should typically be reserved for couple time, this might be an occasion to get some other friends involved. Here are just a few possibilities:*

- *Go to a karaoke club and sing a duet together. Wow the crowd as you belt out your favorite torch song!*
- *Take some ballroom dancing lessons, or if you'd rather just wing it, go find a place that offers ballroom dancing and cut a rug together.*
- *Host a game night with some other married couples. Rather than resorting to the typical guys-versus-gals model, play games in which each married couple works together as a team.*

 QUESTIONS: *What are some famous teams you admire? (Note: We're not just talking sports teams here.) What about these famous teams is inspiring? What makes them work well together? What are some practical steps we can take to ensure that we're always working as a team?*

3 THERE'S ALWAYS SOMETHING MORE TO LEARN

The cure for boredom is curiosity.
There is no cure for curiosity.
—Dorothy Parker

THERE IS ALWAYS SOMETHING NEW to learn about your spouse. Always. No matter how long you've been married, no matter how much you think you know about the person you married, you haven't even scratched the surface.

The goal in marriage, then, is not to learn everything there is to learn about your spouse. We've already established that it isn't possible. It's important, however, to continually be a *student* of your spouse. This is a lifelong process. You may never know everything there is to know, but it's important to update your knowledge at every opportunity. That same sense of discovery you had during your time of premarital dating is possible now. You just need to remain curious!

ACTIVITY: *During this date, what you say—what you discuss—may be more important than the activity itself. So feel free to engage in a typical dating activity, such as going out for a nice dinner or*

*playing a round of miniature golf or just taking a romantic walk
in the park.*

*On the other hand, you may consider creating an activity
that stimulates your curiosity. For example, you could plan your
date around the famous ice-breaker game Two Truths and a Lie.
Each of you writes down three statements about yourself, two
of which are true and one of which isn't. Then during your date,
exchange your statements and see if your spouse can figure out
which statement about you isn't true.*

*Of course, under normal circumstances we wouldn't advo-
cate that you and your spouse lie to each other! If the thought of
"lying" in this way, even in the name of good fun, is uncomfortable to you, simply create a quiz about yourself that your spouse
can answer during the date. You'd be surprised how challenging
such an activity can be, even with seemingly obvious questions
like "What is my favorite food?" "What is my favorite movie?"
or "What is my favorite color?" See how many questions your
spouse can answer before he or she gets tripped up!*

QUESTIONS: *After completing the Two Truths and a Lie game or
taking your quiz, discuss the following Questions: What one
thing did you learn about me tonight that you didn't know before? What are some practical steps we can take to stay current
with each other? What does it mean for us to be students of
each other?*

4 RANDOM ACTS
OF KINDNESS

....

Three things in human life are important:
the first is to be kind; the second is to be
kind; and the third is to be kind.
—Henry James

DO YOU MAKE AN EFFORT to be kind to each other,
simply for the sake of being kind? Married couples
often fall into the routine of doing nice things for
one another only when it's absolutely necessary or,
even worse, as a way of coercing their partner into
something. For example, there's nothing wrong
with a gift on your spouse's birthday, but let's face it,
that's what is expected of you.

The type of kindness we have in mind is the
self-sacrificing, giving, "just because I love you" type
of kindness that isn't coercive and doesn't expect
something in return. These don't have to be huge,
expensive "events." They can be simple everyday
activities that convey your love and appreciation
to your spouse. It might be helping put the kids to
bed—or even handling the bedtime routine all by
yourself without being asked to do so—even though
that's typically your spouse's responsibility. It might
be calling to remind your spouse that you're praying
for him or her—or even praying together over the

phone—on a day when an important meeting is taking place at work. In marriage, the most important acts of kindness are those unprompted, simple gestures of love that say "I love you, I'm thinking about you, and I care about you" on a daily basis.

ACTIVITY: *Go out for dinner and then pick another fun date activity—perhaps bowling or visiting an amusement park or an arcade. Over the course of the date, make every effort to be extra thoughtful and courteous toward your spouse. Enjoy the experience of simply being kind to each other. Don't be disingenuous about it, but don't be afraid to lay it on thick either.*

QUESTIONS: *After your activity is over, go somewhere quiet and enjoy a time of conversing and connecting. Discuss the following Questions: What are some of the "little things" I did for you on our date that you appreciated? Over the course of a typical week, how do I demonstrate my love for you? What else can I do in the future?*

Be sure to keep your answers uplifting and affirming. The idea isn't to criticize your spouse in the areas where he or she is falling short. The goal is to affirm what he or she is already doing, to exchange ideas, and to offer helpful suggestions for the future.

5 THE BLESSING

....

> *Nothing tears down a marriage or family like*
> *criticism, and nothing builds and restores it*
> *like words of encouragement and praise.*
> —Dr. Steve Stephens, *The Wounded Woman*

SINCE IT WAS FIRST PUBLISHED in 1990, millions of
readers have been impacted by Dr. John Trent and
Dr. Gary Smalley's book *The Blessing*. (A shout-out to
Greg's dad!) Based on numerous examples in Scripture,
including those involving God the Father blessing His
children, "the blessing" includes five elements:[1]

1. *Meaningful and appropriate touch.* This is
   key to communicating warmth, acceptance,
   and affirmation.
2. *Spoken words.* To see the blessing grow in
   someone's life, "we need to verbalize our
   message."[2] Blessing-filled *words* communicate genuine acceptance.
3. *Expressing high value.* In blessing one of his
   sons, Isaac said, "[His scent] is like the smell
   of a field that the Lord has blessed" (Gen-
   esis 27:27). "Word pictures are a powerful
   way of communicating acceptance."[3]
4. *Picturing a special future.* Throughout Scripture, God "goes to great lengths to assure us
   of our present relationship with Him and of

the ocean full of blessings in store for us as His children."[4] We need to picture just such a special future for our loved ones if we are serious about giving them our blessing.

5. *An active commitment.* "Words alone cannot communicate the blessing; they need to be backed with a commitment to do everything possible to help the one blessed be successful."[5]

ACTIVITY: *If you're not familiar with the concept of the blessing, track down a copy of the original book, or better yet, find The Gift of the Blessing,[6] which includes a chapter written exclusively with married couples in mind. If possible, read the relevant sections before your date so you'll be familiar with the concepts by the time your date night arrives. Then, either over dinner or at your favorite coffee shop, or in another quiet location, host your own two-person Blessing Discussion Group.*

QUESTIONS: *As you discuss incorporating the blessing into your marriage, be sure to address the following Questions: Did you feel blessed by your parents? Why or why not? What do I do that blesses you? How can we further incorporate the five elements of the blessing into our marriage?*

---

6 A VALENTINE'S
DAY DATE

. . . .

I think that men know how to romance a woman,
and most do it well, at least for a time, otherwise
women wouldn't marry them. The problem is
that most of them begin to rest on their laurels.
—Nicholas Sparks

AH, VALENTINE'S DAY. IT'S A holiday that can paralyze
men with the fear of not living up to their wife's
expectations. However, our culture makes it easy
to celebrate this holiday devoted to romantic love.
Face it: In its modern incarnation, Valentine's Day is
essentially a shopping tradition kept alive by florists
and greeting-card and candy companies. (Considering the fact that Valentine chocolates start appearing
on store shelves literally the day after Christmas,
it's amazing that so many men still fail to remember Valentine's Day after the nearly two months of
marketing that precede it!)

Now, don't get us wrong. We're not anti–
Valentine's Day. Any holiday that encourages couples
to turn toward each other and devote attention to
the romantic aspects of their relationship is fine by
us. However, when it comes to married couples, Valentine's Day can create a problem. Thriving relationships need far more than one day per year devoted

to expressions of romantic love. If you're saving all your romantic gestures for February 14th, while the rest of the year is just the "same old, same old," your relationship likely won't survive. It's as simple as that. Your spouse needs to be reminded, reassured, and encouraged in your love for him or her on a regular and consistent basis, all year, every year.

ACTIVITY: *If a romantic dinner on February 14th is your annual tradition, by all means, go for it! However, you might also consider doing something outside the norm. While everyone else is dining by candlelight, perhaps the two of you could play laser tag or go fishing! Who says activities like these can't be romantic? Sometimes doing something new, exciting, and unexpected can create more vivid memories than repeating the same thing year after year.*

QUESTIONS: *Because Valentine's Day is an annual event, it presents a great opportunity for reminiscing. Either during your activity or in a quiet location afterward, take some time to remember and reflect upon your previous Valentine's Days together. Discuss the following Questions: Do you remember our first Valentine's Day together? What did we do last year for Valentine's Day? Let's see if we can make a list, by year, of all our Valentine's Day dates up to this point.*

---

7 SHARED INTERESTS

Friendship . . . is born at the moment when
one [person] says to another, "What! You too?
I thought that no one but myself . . ."
—C. S. Lewis, *The Four Loves*

IT'S A COMMON THEME FOR many married couples.
He likes to do "guy stuff" like playing sports,
collecting baseball cards, or going hunting. She likes
"girly stuff" like scrapbooking, sewing, or blogging
about bargains. Certainly, some of these activities
speak to the innate differences between males and
females. It would be a serious mistake, however, for
couples to assume that every moment of free time
should be relegated to "his interests" and "her interests," and never the twain shall meet.

Having common hobbies can help couples
deepen their sense of intimacy, connection, and
especially *friendship*. When was the last time you
thought about your spouse as your friend—someone you enjoy spending time with and with whom
you can engage in mutually satisfying pursuits? If
husbands and wives have a firm grasp of their roles
as partners, lovers, or parents but fail to understand
what it means to be friends, they're missing out on
a key component of marriage. The Bible places
the concept of friendship front and center in King

Solomon's depiction of romantic love: "This is my lover, this [is] my *friend*" (Song of Songs 5:16).

ACTIVITY: *Choosing a new restaurant is a fantastic way for husbands and wives to develop a common interest. Find a restaurant or a type of cuisine that neither of you has tried before. You'll experience something new together for the first time. And who knows? You both just might like it! If you have time prior to your date, google "date-night ideas," "hobbies for married couples," or a similar phrase to identify potential activities that you might enjoy together. The idea is not only to select a new and exciting activity for your date but also to identify a hobby or pastime the two of you, as a couple, can return to again and again as a shared interest. The possibilities are endless, but here are just a few activities you might consider: cycling, bird watching, coauthoring a blog, collecting antiques or artwork, composing music together or jamming on instruments, photography, clay modeling or pottery, scuba diving, horseback riding, learning a form of self-defense, "treasure hunting" with a metal detector, gardening or landscaping, cooking, or volunteering at church or with a local social-service agency.*

QUESTIONS: *After your activity, discuss the following Questions: What were some of your favorite hobbies as a child? Have any of those hobbies retained your interest as an adult? What are some of the key things that make your favorite hobbies enjoyable? Do you prefer activities that are more physical in nature,* *or those that provide a mental challenge? What hobby would you pursue if time and money weren't factors?*

The final, and most important, question for you to discuss is this: Did both of you truly enjoy your shared experience? Remember, the purpose of a shared interest isn't to let one spouse be a martyr for the sake of the other, suffering through something that he or she truly doesn't enjoy, but to identify and cultivate activities that both spouses genuinely enjoy doing together.

---

8 WINDSHIELD TIME!

Stop worrying about the potholes in the
road and celebrate the journey.
—attributed to Barbara Hoffman

ACCORDING TO A 2009 DEPARTMENT of Transportation survey, the average adult spent almost a *full hour* in the car every day.[1] We can all relate to that, right? Whether it's the daily commute to and from work, a hectic schedule of taxiing kids to school and other activities, or running errands, driving is a significant part of our everyday experience.

The question is, *How do you use that time?*

When it comes to drive time with your spouse, embrace the opportunity to connect through conversation. It's about *enjoying* the drive rather than simply getting through it. You may be just making a quick trip to the grocery store. But those few moments in the car—something that seems so basic and routine—represent an opportunity for you and your spouse to share your feelings and connect. That's windshield time!

Whether it's your regular date or any other time you and your spouse spend together in the car . . . *it's not just about the destination; it's about the journey*!

DATE 8

ACTIVITY: *To help you get more comfortable with the idea of connecting with your spouse while driving, the majority of this month's date will be spent in your car. Just drive and enjoy having the extra time to connect with each other. Here are some ideas:*

- *Don't be afraid to venture outside the city limits. Drive to a neighboring city for dinner.*
- *Are there any scenic byways in your area? Are there out-of-the-way back roads known for their sightseeing potential? Explore the world around you.*
- *If you'll be driving after dark, find out whether there are any roads that overlook the city lights. There's nothing like taking in a romantic cityscape!*

 QUESTIONS: *Remember, the purpose of windshield time is to learn how to connect with meaningful conversation while you're in the car, not to drive for driving's sake. Here are some possible questions to discuss:*

- *What are some ways I can show you I'm interested in you and want to know you better?*
- *What are some ways I can more effectively communicate that I love you?*
- *Did you go on family drives as a child? How did that time make you feel?*
- *Out of all the date nights we've experienced together thus far, which one has been your favorite? Why?*

9 PASSION

*Boys and girls in America have such a sad time
together; sophistication demands that they submit
to sex immediately without proper preliminary talk.
Not courting talk—real straight talk about souls,
for life is holy and every moment is precious.*
—Jack Kerouac, *On the Road*

EVEN BEAT POET JACK KEROUAC understood that
human sexuality is special—and sacred. It involves
not only the body but the soul. It represents the
pinnacle of human connection and is not to be
taken lightly.

If that's the case, then why is it so difficult for
married couples to enjoy a thriving sexual relationship as the years go by? We may believe in our
heads that sex with our spouse is important, but it's
incredibly difficult to give it the priority it deserves.
When we do find the time, the experience is often
routine and mundane—just another item to check
off the list. One study found that due to jobs, kids,
hobbies, family responsibilities, and other factors,
the average married couple spends just *four minutes
a day* alone together.[1] Four minutes! That's barely
enough time to say hello, let alone engage in meaningful physical intimacy.

And that's what this date is all about—*intimacy*,

of which sex is only one expression. Dictionary.com defines *intimacy* as "a close, familiar, and usually affectionate or loving personal relationship with another person or group."[2] Did you catch that? Closeness. Familiarity. Affection. Love. Isn't that what marriage is all about?

ACTIVITY: *Order in and enjoy a great meal and conversation in the comfort of your own home. Light some candles and put out a tablecloth, even if you'll be eating only out of your to-go containers. Light candles in the bedroom, the living room, and other areas where you'll be spending time as well. Break out your wedding album or video and reminisce about the special events of that day. Celebrate the journey that has brought you from that day to today. Put on some romantic music that will help set a relaxed, romantic mood. Even though you won't be leaving the house, be sure to put effort into looking attractive for your spouse.*

QUESTIONS: *Asking each other questions—that's not very sexy, is it? It certainly can be! Take turns talking with your spouse about the physical features you find particularly appealing in him or her. Be specific! And what about nonphysical characteristics? Are you attracted to your spouse's sense of humor? Intellect? Compassionate heart? Let him or her know!*

Be sure to flavor these conversations with plenty of cuddling, kissing, and so on. Engage in nonsexual touching, such as back rubs and foot massages. Enjoy being in close physical proximity without feeling the need to jump right into the "main event."

As the evening has progressed, hopefully you and your spouse have begun to feel closer and more connected. This closeness—this intimacy*—has likely produced in both of you a desire to connect sexually. As you and your spouse enter this phase of the evening, ask yourselves the following Questions: Is there anything specific we can do to "spice up" our sex life and add some variety? How can I be more giving toward you during sex?*

Keep in mind that the idea isn't to engage in activities that are uncomfortable for either partner. If you try something new (or that hasn't been a part of your repertoire for a while), make sure it's mutually agreed upon and edifying to both partners.

The cliché is that after sex, the man will roll over and go to sleep while the woman lies awake, wishing for additional time to cuddle, talk, and connect. Husbands, here's your chance to shatter that stereotype! Spend some additional time connecting emotionally and physically with your wife.

10 I CHERISH YOU

Where your treasure is, there
your heart will be also.
—Matthew 6:21

ACCORDING TO MERRIAM-WEBSTER ONLINE DICTIONARY,
cherish means "to hold dear,"[1] to regard someone
or something as a treasure. This comes naturally to
those who are caught up in the first flush of youth-
ful romantic love. But feelings can fade over time,
and when that happens, cherishing can survive and
thrive only if it graduates to a higher level. It needs
to be lifted out of the realm of mere emotion and
transformed into a steady, consistent attitude. It has
to become an intentional act of the will.

I (Greg) saw the beauty of the "cherish list"
in action a few years ago when Erin and I spent
Thanksgiving at my parents' home in Branson,
Missouri. At one point, my folks got into a huge
argument. (Yes, it happens in the elder Smalley
household. One of the things I admire about my
parents' marriage is that they don't claim to have
a "perfect" relationship, and they're not afraid to
disagree.) This particular disagreement was a doozy,
to the point that my folks retired to opposite ends of
the house for a while. I ventured into my dad's study
later to see how he was doing. I found him sitting

behind his computer and assumed he was catching up on the news or weather. Instead, he was reading a document he had created called "Why Norma Is So Valuable" (that's my mom's name). The list contained literally hundreds of words and phrases describing my mom's value. It was astonishing!

I asked him about it, and he said, "Years ago I started a list of reasons why your mom is so valuable. When I'm upset with her or when we've had a fight, instead of sitting here thinking about how hurt or frustrated I am, I make myself read through this list. The more I read, the faster I realize that you have an amazing mom." That's the power of cherishing your mate!

ACTIVITY: Before *your date, each of you should take some time alone to make a list of the things you value about your spouse. Include his or her personality traits, character qualities, spirituality, caring behaviors, accomplishments, and even physical characteristics. Write them down and take the list with you on your date. Then, over dinner or in a quiet location, share your cherish lists with each other. Don't simply hand your list to your spouse and expect him or her to read it in silence. Instead, actually* read *your list aloud.*

After you've shared your list, give it to your spouse and, if time allows, consider going to a scrapbook or craft store to get some stickers or even picture frames to adorn your lists.

Keeping the list you've been given in a wallet or purse, on the nightstand, or in another easily seen location will remind you regularly of the reasons your spouse cherishes you.

QUESTIONS: *After you've exchanged your cherish lists, answer the following Questions: What was your favorite part of the evening? What is one thing you learned about me tonight that you didn't know before? What is one way I can let you know I cherish you during the coming week?*

---

11 I FEEL LOVED
WHEN YOU . . .

*It's not who I am underneath, but
what I do that defines me.*
—Batman, in *Batman Begins*

BATMAN KNOWS THAT BEING A superhero involves
more than just talking about the importance of
truth and justice. It's not simply believing in the
right things. At some point, those beliefs and feelings have to translate into something tangible. This
principle applies to marriage as well. You may have
deep feelings of love for your spouse in your heart,
and you may even express those feelings in words
on a regular basis. But at some point, those feelings
need to be put into *action*!

To express your love in tangible ways is to
nourish your spouse. It's closely related to *cherishing*.
Both disciplines are drawn from the apostle Paul's
letter to the church at Ephesus, when he wrote, "No
one ever hated his own flesh, but *nourishes* and *cherishes* it, just as Christ also does the church" (Ephe-
sians 5:29, NASB). "Cherishing," as described in the
previous date, is an *attitude* that involves recognizing
your mate's inherent value. "Nourishing," on the
other hand, is an *action* in which you treat your
spouse in ways that show you value him or her.

During the previous date, you developed a list of the traits and characteristics you admire about your spouse and shared that list with him or her. Now you're going to breathe life into those thoughts and emotions and *nourish* each other.

ACTIVITY: *Either over dinner or in a quiet location, talk about ways you can nourish each other spiritually, emotionally, and physically. Get a pen and paper and write down your ideas, starting with the phrase "I feel loved when you . . ." For example, I feel loved when you . . .*

> *pray with me.*
> *provide positive affirmation.*
> *act curious about me.*
> *show affection.*
> *have fun and laugh with me.*

Once you've completed your lists, exchange them and talk about them. If there's time, you might engage in a simple activity that will help you put the idea of nourishing into practice. For example:

- *Go bowling and be sure to provide each other with lots of positive affirmation (even if your spouse's ball continually ends up in the gutter!).*
- *Go to a movie and use the time as an opportunity to be affectionate—hold hands, put your arm around your wife, etc.*

- *Go to a secluded location, even if just sitting in the
   car, and pray together. Make an effort to connect on a
   spiritual level.*

QUESTIONS: *After your activity, discuss the following Questions:
What was your favorite part of the evening? What was one thing
you learned about me on our date? What are some other ways I
can nourish you in the days and weeks ahead?*

12 HOLY

If God had the gospel of Jesus's salvation
in mind when he established marriage,
then marriage only "works" to the degree
that [it] approximates the pattern of
God's self-giving love in Christ.
—Timothy Keller, *The Meaning of Marriage*

DO YOU AND YOUR SPOUSE feel as if you're growing together spiritually? Many couples not only struggle to build physical, emotional, and relational intimacy in their marriages (hence the need for regular date nights!), but they also discover that it's tough to be *spiritually* intimate with each other. The reasons for this are similar to the reasons why it's tough to build intimacy in other areas: limited time; a too-busy lifestyle; the demands of childrearing, career, and, yes, even church. Most of us struggle to have just a few minutes of personal prayer and Bible reading on a regular basis, let alone find time to pray or study Scripture with our spouses! Like cultivating romance with your beloved, fostering spiritual growth—both individually and in your marriage—takes discipline and intentionality. It won't just happen.

For the purposes of this date, we'll assume that you and your spouse are roughly in the same

ballpark when it comes to your Christian walk.
The goal of this date will be to help you "encourage
one another—and all the more as you see the Day
approaching" (Hebrews 10:25).

ACTIVITY: *Do you view your dates as opportunities to invite
God into your activities—and not just with a quick "Thank
You, Lord, for this food" before dinner? Your dates represent
a wonderful opportunity for you to dig deep and connect
spiritually as a couple. For this date, consider one of the
following activities to help direct your thoughts heavenward:
Attend a Christian concert; visit a museum or exhibit dedicated
to religious art, Christian iconography, or biblical history; go
for a hike and consider God's handiwork in nature; reach out
to someone in Jesus' name—volunteer at a soup kitchen or a
homeless shelter.*

QUESTIONS: *The real meat of this date will become evident
in your discussion. After your activity, explore some of the
following Questions: How would you share your testimony with
me if I were a new acquaintance? What one person in your life
has been most influential in shaping your view of God? How can
I pray for you? What have you been learning during your times
of personal prayer and Scripture reading? What recent sermons
have impacted you at church?*

*Most important, ask yourselves this: How can we continue
to help each other grow spiritually on a regular basis? The*

purpose of this date isn't to have a one-time spiritual discus-
sion and then return to your regular routine. It's about making
spiritual intimacy a regular feature of your marriage. Create
a game plan for how you can both devote regular, consistent
time to growing together *spiritually, as well as encouraging and*
building each other up (see 1 Thessalonians 5:11).

13 REMEMBER WHEN . . .

Sweet memories, of holding hands and
red bouquets, of twilight trimmed in
purple haze, and laughing eyes . . .
—"Memories," performed by Elvis Presley

WE'VE ALREADY ESTABLISHED THAT ONE of the best
ways for couples to build intimacy is through *remi-*
niscing. Remembering and celebrating special times
in your relationship are very important. Often when
we think of reminiscing, we tend to frame it in the
context of remembering those really *big* events from
marriage—our wedding day, the birth of a child, a
dream vacation, and so on.

But what about the little things? Sometimes,
the sweetest, most tender memories are those that
happened during unplanned moments that may
seem unremarkable to the casual observer. Think
about some of those times in your own marriage:
doing the dishes or other household chores together,
working in the garden together, or just sitting on
the front step on warm summer evenings watching
the neighborhood wind down. These are typical
daily occurrences, but when viewed from the present
looking back, they can carry an added sense of peace
and connection between you and your spouse.

DATE 13

Embrace this date as an opportunity for you and your spouse to remember some of your happiest times together, whether big events or simple everyday activities. As C. S. Lewis wrote, "A pleasure is full grown only when it is remembered."[1]

 ACTIVITY: *We live in a mobile society, so statistically, the chances aren't great that you still live near the old haunts you visited during your dating or courtship. Some couples move several times within their first few years of marriage! Nevertheless, if you do still have access to some of the places you frequented during the early years of your relationship, why don't you visit them again? And even if you've moved away, you can improvise. Maybe you had a favorite coffee shop in Des Moines when you first met during your college years. Now that you live in Sacramento, see if you can find a similar coffee shop that will help you relive that experience.*

 QUESTIONS: *What are some favorite things we used to do as a couple early in our marriage? Can we start doing some of those things again, even with the realities of our busier lifestyle? Name two special memories you cherish that have nothing to do with the big events of our relationship (the wedding, childbirth, etc.). Why are those memories so special to you?*

---

14 LAUGH WITH ME

Among those whom I like or admire,
I can find no common denominator,
but among those whom I love, I can;
all of them make me laugh.
—W. H. Auden

DO YOU EVER WONDER WHY so many personal ads, from both men and women, seek a partner with a good sense of humor, or someone who loves to laugh? Because laughter is attractive! This is true at the beginning of a relationship, and it's true after years of marriage. An article in *Scientific American* notes that "when seeking a mate, men desire women who laugh at their jokes, whereas women prefer men who can make them laugh."[1] After a relationship is established, the role of laughter changes, but it's no less important. For example, women in committed relationships value laughter and humor for their ability to "relieve tense discussions."[2]

Consider these important benefits associated with laughter:

- Laughter contributes to normal blood flow. The University of Maryland conducted a study in which some subjects watched a funny movie while others watched a drama. Afterward, those who had watched the comedy demonstrated normal blood flow in their vessels, while those who had watched the drama had tensed up, restricting blood flow.[3]

- Laughter boosts your immunity. Studies show that laughter may boost the body's ability to fight infection.[4]
- Laughter contributes to better relaxation and satisfying sleep.[5]

You probably know from experience that laughter can help improve relationships as well. Think of some of your favorite times with family and friends. Chances are, many of those memories involve moments of fun and laughter. The ability to laugh together helps us bond with one another!

 ACTIVITY: *The success of this date depends on your knowing each other well enough to understand what your partner finds funny. It could be something as simple as sitting across the table from each other and telling funny stories. Or it could involve something more adventurous, such as going to a comedy club or a funny movie. You might also consider visiting a bookstore or going online and finding a book of clean jokes or Mad Libs.*

 QUESTIONS: *Ask each other these Questions: What makes you laugh? What about our activity did you find particularly funny?*

Also talk about the art of laughing at yourself. Are there some silly or funny quirks about your spouse that you find irresistibly funny? Maybe her set of 1950s-vintage hair curlers, or his Snoopy boxer shorts? Be sure to pick things that are lighthearted and fun. Don't laugh at your spouse's expense or be cruel.

15 THEY'RE JUST LIKE TWO KIDS IN LOVE . . .

We don't stop playing because we grow old;
we grow old because we stop playing.
—George Bernard Shaw

WHEN WAS THE LAST TIME you felt like you played?
For most of us, playtime is a vestige of childhood.
We left it behind when we entered the world of
adulthood. Respectable folks who are raising kids,
holding down jobs, serving at church, and making
meaningful contributions to society don't play, do
they? After all, the apostle Paul himself said, "When
I was a child, I talked like a child, I thought like
a child, I reasoned like a child. When I became a
man, I put childish ways behind me" (1 Corinthians
13:11). Hrrumph!

We certainly don't question the authority of
Paul's words, which are the inspired Word of God.
But if that verse hangs over your head as an admo-
nition against having fun or taking time to play and
recreate, then we'd suggest that 1 Corinthians 13:11
doesn't mean quite what you think it means.

Within reason there's nothing wrong with re-
sponsible, upstanding adults having fun and engaging in leisurely activities from time to time. These
pursuits are actually essential to your emotional

and mental health. And there's certainly a case to be made for husbands and wives enjoying playtime *together* on occasion. That's what this date is all about.

 ACTIVITY: *You can both probably name some things you like to do when it comes to leisure activities. You're certainly free to select something from your current list of favorites that you'd both find enjoyable. But to make things more interesting, why not consider something you haven't done for a while—maybe for a long while? Maybe not even since you were kids? Talk about some of your favorite childhood playtime activities and then consider incorporating one or more of them into your date. Here are some examples:*

- *Go to a ball game. Make sure to eat lots of peanuts and ice cream.*
- *Go to an amusement park. Load up on hot dogs and cotton candy—but ride the roller coaster first!*
- *Find an old board game or even a set of marbles and play a few rounds together.*
- *Have a tea party complete with fancy cups and saucers. Instead of serving tea to your dollies, serve each other.*

QUESTIONS: *This date presents a great opportunity to dig a little deeper into any preconceptions you may have about leisure time. Discuss the following Questions: What were some of your favorite things to play as a child? How did your family view playtime? Was it frowned upon or encouraged?*

Read Ecclesiastes chapter 3 together ("There is a time for everything and a season for every activity under heaven . . ." [verse 1]). Then discuss these Questions: Do you think leisure time fits into this passage somewhere? How can we be more intentional about including reasonable amounts of playtime in our schedule?

16 SWEAT

I like to move it, move it. She likes to
move it, move it. He likes to move it,
move it. You like to—move it!)
—"I Like to Move It," from *Madagascar*

IN 2011 THE BUREAU OF Labor Statistics found that the amount of time people (fifteen years of age and older) engaged in a sports or exercise activity on an average day in the United States was eighteen minutes. But the time people spent watching TV on an average day was almost *ten times* that amount![1]

While it's certainly true that many Americans seem to have an aversion to physical activity and eschew it altogether, others carry exercise to the opposite extreme. A study in the *Mayo Clinic Proceedings*, for example, found that while people who exercise regularly enjoy tremendous health benefits, those who train hard for triathlons, ultramarathons, and other extreme events run a much greater risk of suffering serious heart damage.[2]

There has to be a happy medium somewhere, right? It's somewhere between having a heart attack because you're a couch potato and having a heart attack because you're an extreme-sports junkie. Why not consider making exercise a shared activity?

DATE 16

ACTIVITY: *If you typically go to a gym to work out, take your spouse along this time. Teach your spouse your workout routine. If time and circumstances allow, do something more ambitious. Try something you haven't done before, such as rock climbing or kayaking. If you'd like to engage in something more long term together, consider training for a half marathon or registering for a local charity run.*

 BONUS ACTIVITY: *Many people use fast-paced music to exercise. When you have some free time, create a workout "playlist" together that includes some of your and your spouse's favorite workout songs. Then make sure the playlist is available on both of your devices. This is a great way to be reminded of your spouse the next time you're working out on your own.*

 QUESTIONS: *After your activity (and perhaps a shower and a bottle of Gatorade!), discuss the following Questions: How important is physical fitness to you? How can we encourage each other (and our kids) in the pursuit of a balanced approach to physical fitness—not too lax and not too extreme? During our physical activity, what was one thing you learned about me that you didn't know before?*

17 LOOKING FORWARD

Life can only be understood backwards;
but it must be lived forwards.
—Søren Kierkegaard

WHAT WILL YOUR MARRIAGE LOOK like one year from now? How about two years? Ten years? At the beginning of this chapter, you enjoyed a New Year's date, during which you looked ahead to the coming year and set goals for your relationship and your marriage. Now it's time to take that same concept and cast a longer-term vision for the future.

This process isn't about making concrete plans or administrating the next decade of your relationship. Carrying this concept too far will only lead to frustration, and besides, it's not biblical.

The years ahead in your marriage will bring many unexpected blessings, and many unexpected trials. They will be filled with events and occurrences for which you simply couldn't have planned. That's part of the deal. It's also one of the reasons you made a commitment on your wedding day to love each other "for better or for worse." You simply don't know what forms the better and the worse will take until they reveal themselves in the course of God's good timing.

What you *can* do, though, is set goals for your relationship that will help you grow closer and more intimate throughout the remaining years of your marriage, through the good and bad times that are sure to come. Together you can embrace God's awesome promise: "I know the plans I have for you . . . plans to prosper you and not to harm you, plans to give you hope and a future" (Jeremiah 29:11).

ACTIVITY: *For your New Year's date, we recommended that you engage in a morning activity, such as going out for breakfast or taking an invigorating hike. We'd like to suggest a morning activity for this date as well. In our experience, thinking, praying, and casting a vision for the future are easier to do under sunny skies at the start of a new day than they are in the dark of night. So get up, go outdoors, and breathe in the possibilities!*

QUESTIONS: *After your activity, sit down and talk about your future together. How do we envision our future together? What aspects of our relationship do we want to enhance together on the road ahead? You might even consider writing a marriage mission statement together. Talk about your shared vision and values for your relationship, and then craft a brief, simple statement together that encapsulates those values. For example, "We will pursue intimacy with God and with each other for the sake of our children, the world around us, and the glory of God."*

---

18 SPRUCING
UP THE NEST

The sun at home warms better
than the sun elsewhere.
—Albanian proverb

ONE OF THE POINTS WE'VE been trying to make
throughout this book is that in addition to carving out time for dating, husbands and wives have
the opportunity to build intimacy through their
everyday activities. It's true: Doing household chores
doesn't automatically bring to mind romance. But
there's no reason these activities have to be routine
and mundane. They're mindless chores only if
you allow them to be. So pick something around
the house that needs doing, and *do it*! But do it
together, and make it fun.

Here's an example from our own experience:
One time when we were folding laundry together,
Erin went up to get some more dirty clothes from
the kids' rooms. While she was upstairs, the washing
machine finished, and I (Greg) went to unload it.
I noticed our five-year-old daughter standing next
to me, begging to help. A devilish plan formed in
my mind. Without really considering the conse-
quences or possible dangers, I talked my daughter
into hiding in the empty dryer. I then waited for

DATE 18

Erin. When she returned, she dropped the dirty clothes into the laundry basket and took the clean load out of the washing machine. I silently peeked around the corner and watched her move toward the dryer. When Erin opened the door to throw in the wet clothes, our daughter screamed and grabbed her arm. It was awesome! Erin jumped about four feet in the air and ran out of the laundry room screaming. I'll spare you the ugly details—let's just say that I ended up doing the rest of the laundry by myself. But you know what? It turned a mundane chore into something fun that we still laugh about today—even Erin.

ACTIVITY: *Paint a room, put up wallpaper, install carpet, clean out the basement—anything that will spruce up your house. Have fun investing in the beauty of your home, making it a fun and inviting space that lends itself to building happy memories. Turn what could be a mundane chore or a looming responsibility into a fun chance to connect.*

And here's something that will definitely make the process more interesting (and appealing): At the end of your project, you'll likely be dirty. You may have paint all over your face or grime in your hair, or you may just be good and sweaty. Why don't you resolve to help each other clean up after your project is finished (and after the kids are in bed)? Perhaps you can take a hot bath or shower together to help scrub all those hard-to-reach places on your partner. Then you can head to bed to massage all the sore muscles your spouse developed during the project. Who knows what other activities might come to mind as you endeavor to unwind from your house beautifying project!

QUESTIONS: *As you work on your home-improvement project, share memories of your childhoods and the roles that your living spaces played in those memories. Ask each other these Questions: What specific rooms, pieces of furniture, colors, or designs made an impression on you in your childhood home? What special memories do you have of your living space as a child? How important is our home environment now to creating good memories for us and our children?*

19 LISTEN UP!

My wife says I never listen to her. At
least I think that's what she said.
—Author unknown

COMMUNICATION IS A KEY INGREDIENT in any healthy marriage. And one of the most important components of good communication is *listening*. The Bible reminds us that we are to be "quick to listen, slow to speak and slow to become angry" (James 1:19).

The simple act of listening—of actually hearing and absorbing what your spouse is saying—conveys several important messages. It signifies that you want to *understand* your spouse not just in terms of the words being used but in terms of the feelings behind those words. Listening also helps you *validate* your spouse. As a rule, your mate will only desire to communicate with you to the degree that he or she feels heard and understood. Finally, listening helps you develop *empathy* for your spouse. Empathy goes beyond "I understand what you're feeling" and says, "I feel what you're feeling."

ACTIVITY: *You may be tempted to say, "Uh-oh, Greg and Erin. We're talking about communication and empathy now. That*

sounds very, um, 'diagnostic.' Are we going to break the rules you set forth and start administrating our dates?"

Don't worry, we're not going to get all "marriage counselor" on you. For this date, pick a fun activity that you both enjoy, such as going out for a nice dinner, bowling, to a coffee shop, or to the ballet. Or go see a movie or a play that you can discuss afterward—you know, so that you can put those communication skills to work! As always, have fun!

QUESTIONS: *Even within the context of a fun date, there's no reason why you can't talk about your marital communication skills in an uplifting, positive manner. After your activity, talk about ways you can communicate more effectively. This isn't a time to berate or criticize your spouse; it's simply an opportunity to invest in healthy communication, which will in turn deepen your intimacy. Ask yourselves, "What are some ways we can more effectively incorporate understanding, validation, and empathy into our communication as a couple?"*

20 REST

God made time, but man made haste.
—Irish proverb

BEING BUSY ALL DAY EVERY day robs us of quality time with our families. It erects a barrier to important couple time and intimacy. Rushing headlong from one commitment to the next creates stress, which can become overwhelming and even debilitating. In fact, WebMD reports that stress contributes to headaches, high blood pressure, heart problems, diabetes, asthma, and depression, among other problems. Studies show that "stress-related ailments and complaints" comprise between 75 and 90 percent of all doctor's office visits![1]

You also need to know that if you're living at a frantic pace, you're potentially doing damage to your kids as well. How's that for a guilt trip? A Finnish study found that the children of parents who suffer from burnout are more likely to suffer from burnout themselves.[2] This is really just common sense. We already know that we have the greatest influence on our kids by what we *show* them rather than what we *tell* them.

For the sake of our marriages, and our kids, we must create space in our lives for a little downtime.

ACTIVITY: *Here's your chance to do something spontaneous and relaxed. Whatever you do, make sure you allow plenty of time beforehand so you're not rushing to your destination. You're defeating the purpose if you have to hurry up and relax! The activity itself will depend on what the two of you find especially soothing, but here are a few ideas:*

- *Get a couples' massage from a reputable therapist.*
- *Many Middle Eastern restaurants serve patrons in the traditional style—i.e., sitting on the floor and reclining on pillows, and so on. See if you can find a Moroccan, Afghan, or similar restaurant that offers this relaxing feature.*
- *Stay home and enjoy the feeling of not having to go anywhere! Enjoy a hot bath together or some time in the hot tub. Put on some relaxing music. Cuddle in front of the fireplace.*

 QUESTIONS: *As you relax and unwind together, discuss the following questions: How can we create "margin" in our lives? (Dr. Richard Swenson defines margin as "the space between our load and our limits. . . . Margin is the gap between rest and exhaustion, the space between breathing freely and suffocating."³) Are there unnecessary commitments we can cut out to improve our family's health and vitality? How can we model healthy limits to each other and to our kids?*

2 1   E N C O U R A G E

....

There are two ways of exerting one's strength:
one is pushing down, the other is pulling up.
—Booker T. Washington

THE WORD ENCOURAGE LITERALLY MEANS "to make courageous." It's lifting a person up and affirming him or her to the point that he or she says, "I can do this!" in the face of something that might otherwise seem too challenging.

That's a wonderful picture of what happens in marriage, isn't it? Throughout your relationship, you'll face many struggles, whether unemployment, illness, disease, bankruptcy, childrearing challenges, or just everyday hurts and disappointments. There will be many good times, too, of course. The point is that in marriage, the hills and valleys are easier to take when you have someone in your corner. Out-of-control kids and overwhelming credit-card bills can either tear you apart or pull you closer together. It all depends on your ability to tackle these challenges with a united front. Husbands and wives can *encourage* each other on a date by helping him or her try something new. Have you ever wanted to try something but were too nervous or afraid? Perhaps the activity itself appeals to you, but you've never taken the plunge because you lack confidence. You may feel you just don't have what it takes. It could be a demanding physical activity or something like public speaking or even dancing. If you're willing to be a little adventurous, this date will allow you to indulge that desire as a team, encouraging each other along the way.

ACTIVITY: *If time and budget allow, don't be afraid to go for the gusto here. Try something challenging! Don't put yourselves in any danger, of course, but try to find an activity that lies outside your normal comfort zone. And as you did with the teamwork date earlier, focus on completing it together, offering lots of affirmation to your partner. Here are some possible activities: going skydiving; singing karaoke; participating in a poetry night at a local venue; riding the scariest, most heart-attack-inducing roller coaster you can find.*

QUESTIONS: *After your activity, bring the principles of encouragement back to the real world. You might not jump out of an airplane every day, but you will face challenging situations, whether dealing with unruly kids or with hostile employees or coworkers. Ask your spouse, "How can I encourage you as you face upcoming challenges?" "What do you dread during the week that I can help you face?"*

---

22 TRADITIONS

*What an enormous magnifier is tradition! How a
thing grows in the human memory and in the human
imagination, when love, worship, and all that lies
in the human heart, is there to encourage it.*
—Thomas Carlyle

TRADITIONS ARE AMONG THE BEDROCKS of family life.
When you read the title of this date, it's likely that
a few of your own family traditions immediately
popped into your head. Attending the midnight
service on Christmas Eve, spending a midsummer
weekend at the lake, going on a father-son hunting
trip in the fall. Whatever they are, your family likely
has a handful of special traditions that you hold
dear.

But what about traditions related specifically to
your marriage? Are there any special customs you
and your spouse share and treasure? We're not talking about yearly observances like your anniversary
or birthdays (although those are important). We're
talking about unique events that are important only
to the two of you—things that other folks don't
necessarily understand. Maybe it's having a weekend
getaway, just the two of you, at a favorite nearby
destination. Or perhaps it's something as simple as
going out for coffee on the first Saturday morning

of every month. Whatever the details, maintaining special husband-wife traditions is a great way to build intimacy.

 ACTIVITY: *If you have a cherished couples-only tradition you enjoy, center your date around it! Go out for a nice dinner and plan your next weekend at the mountain chalet. Do you put a complex puzzle together every New Year's Eve? Go to the store now, a few months early, and pick out the puzzle. If you don't have any special traditions as a couple, why not use this opportunity to start one? The possibilities are limited only by your imagination.*

 QUESTIONS: *As you engage in your activity, discuss the following Questions: Did you have special traditions in your family growing up? What were they? What do you remember most about them? How can we create and maintain traditions for our marriage? For our family?*

---

23 TIME FOR A CHECKUP!

There is no more lovely, friendly and
charming relationship, communion or
company than a good marriage.
—Martin Luther

WE'VE SAID MANY TIMES THROUGHOUT this book that
your dates should be characterized by fun; they are
not for administrating your marriage or addressing
problems and conflicts. A couple of the dates thus
far have skirted close to administration territory
without actually crossing over.

This date will be slightly different. It involves
both spouses taking an online assessment known as
Focus on the Family's "Couple Checkup." Each of
you will go to the website *www.focusonthefamily.com
/couplecheckup* and answer roughly 120 questions
related to communication, roles, finances, affection,
conflict, and other aspects of married life. (There's
a one-time $29.95 charge for the checkup, and
there are versions for dating, engaged, and married
couples.)

The "Couple Checkup" is backed by more
than twenty years of research. Focus on the Family's
version has been customized to reflect a distinctly
Christian, or biblical, view of marriage. After each of
you completes the assessment, you'll have a well-

rounded overview of your relationship that will give you insight not only into growth areas but also into your strengths as a couple.

Is taking the "Couple Checkup" the same thing as administrating your marriage? To be honest, yes. There's no point in suggesting otherwise. However, that doesn't mean it has to put a damper on your date-night fun. Think of it as a tool you can use to make your marriage even stronger—to deepen your intimacy with and commitment to each other. Taking the assessment doesn't necessarily suggest that your marriage is in trouble and needs help. Rather, it's a proactive step you can take that signifies a commitment on both of your parts to make your marriage the best it can be.

ACTIVITY: *Prior to your date, each of you should visit* www.focus onthefamily.com/couplecheckup *and take the assessment individually. It typically takes around thirty minutes to complete. Once you've both finished the checkup, print out your results and take them with you on your date. The activity itself can be a nice dinner, a visit to a museum, a walk around the lake, or another activity you both enjoy.*

QUESTIONS: *After your activity is over, go to a quiet location where you can have a hot cup of coffee or another beverage, and pull out your assessments. Discuss the results together.*

Pay attention to those areas in which you're thriving as a couple, as well as those areas that could use some work. Don't be discouraged by any growth areas. Talk about them together and be positive and affirming about ways you can help your relationship grow. Going through the entire assessment may be too much for one date, so commit to completing the process at home or on your next date.

If the process of going through the "Couple Checkup" seems too daunting to accomplish on your own, you might consider getting in touch with another couple you respect, or a pastor, mentor, or even a professional counselor if you believe you need extra help. You can contact Focus on the Family at 1-800-A-FAMILY or www.focusonthefamily.com for assistance in locating a counselor in your area.

24 THE WEEKEND GETAWAY

Come away with me, and we'll kiss on a mountaintop;
come away with me and I'll never stop loving you.
—Norah Jones, "Come Away with Me"

THE WEEKEND GETAWAY TAKES ALL of the dating principles we've been discussing thus far and expands them into a full-blown, multiday event! A regular date night allows you to break free from the common challenges and distractions of home (kids, homework, household chores, etc.) for a few hours of uninterrupted couple time. Getaway weekends are even better. In fact, some marriage experts recommend that husbands and wives schedule at least one or two weekends away *every year*.

Of course, the same challenges to regular date nights (budget concerns, a packed calendar, childcare needs, etc.) are exacerbated when it comes to putting together a weekend getaway. However, with some creativity and determination, we believe that most of these obstacles can be overcome.

ACTIVITY: *Since you'll be away for one or two nights, as well as the better part of two days, you'll have time for plenty of activities. But don't succumb to the temptation to fill every available*

moment with planned events! Sometimes it's best just to get away, relax, and enjoy unstructured downtime. Sleep late. Pray together. Take long walks. Make love. Talk about your hopes and dreams. If you feel up to it, visit some local attractions. Whatever you do, don't let work intrude on your weekend! *Smartphones, iPads, and other devices should be reserved for occasional contact with your children and their caretakers only.*

 QUESTIONS: *If you recently completed Focus on the Family's "Couple Checkup" (see previous date), a weekend getaway would be a great opportunity to talk about some of the things you learned about yourself and your spouse. Don't feel pressure to troubleshoot or solve any perceived problems that you may have discerned after taking the checkup. Rather, accentuate the positive and talk about areas in which you feel you're excelling. Also look back over some of the discussion questions from your previous date nights and see if they lend themselves to deeper conversations than what would have been possible on a standard date night.*

25 VIVE LA DIFFÉRENCE!

*It were not best that we should all think alike; it
is difference of opinion that makes horse races.*
—Mark Twain

EARLIER IN THE CHAPTER WE outlined a date designed to help you and your spouse find common interests—hobbies or activities that you *both* enjoy. That's all well and good, but having areas of shared interest doesn't mean you have to abandon those things that are uniquely you. Guys, you might enjoy watching football, and ladies, you may find scrapbooking to be an invigorating and fulfilling pursuit, but your spouses may never "get it." (Lest you think we're being sexist here, we're sure that many women love watching football and plenty of men relish scrapbooking. Hey, it could happen!) Some of our own diverse interests issues: Erin enjoys these activities: bargain shopping, going on walks with friends, working out, Bible study, watching the series Downton Abbey and romantic comedies, enjoying mocha lattes, working in her flower garden, cooking. Greg, on the other hand, enjoys the following: watching football and other sports, playing video games with the kids, skiing, fishing, working out on the treadmill, watching action movies, and eating!

The point is, it's okay to have interests and

passions that are unique to *you*, even if your spouse doesn't share them. So go ahead and embrace your differences! For this date, you'll pick out two activities—one that appeals uniquely to the husband, and one that appeals uniquely to the wife.

 ACTIVITY: *Here's the deal, though. The purpose of this date isn't to flaunt something you enjoy while your partner is miserable. Nor is the idea to force your spouse into doing something in the hope that he or she will, finally, see the light and enjoy it. Rather, it's to do something you're passionate about to give your spouse a deeper insight into your interests, your personality, and the things that drive you. So pick something you truly enjoy—and let your spouse do the same, either on this date or the next—and then be prepared to discuss and answer questions about why this activity is so important to you.*

 QUESTIONS: *Whatever activities you chose, remember, the point wasn't to make one spouse suffer through something only the other spouse loves. Rather, it was to help you gain an appreciation for your mate's unique interests and passions.*

After your activities are over, discuss the following Questions: Did you find it challenging to engage in my chosen activity? How did it make you feel? Does experiencing it make you appreciate me more?

---

26 STOLEN MOMENTS

Summer's going fast, nights growing
colder; children growing up, old
friends growing older. Freeze this
moment a little bit longer, make
each sensation a little bit stronger.
—Rush, "Time Stand Still"

THE ALARM BUZZES AND THE day begins. You jump out of bed and hit the ground running. You have just enough time to say a quick prayer and read a Bible verse before hitting the shower, getting dressed, and scrambling to the kitchen for breakfast. But don't forget the kids! They also need to get ready for the day—and it's up to you to help make it all happen.

Sound familiar? Most families run through this routine, or something similar, every morning. Your blood pressure is probably rising just thinking about it. And the end of the day isn't any different.

You can't avoid these everyday responsibilities, but what if, for the sake of your marriage, you started to view them as *opportunities* rather than just the day-to-day grind? Is it possible for you and your spouse to experience emotional and relational *connection* in the midst of a busy day? The answer is a resounding *yes!* Whether in the morning or the evening, or even during the day when you're apart, you just need to have a plan for maximizing those everyday moments.

 ACTIVITY: *You know the drill! Do something fun, and if possible, something you haven't tried before. Go to a Nepalese restaurant. Visit the local wax museum. Try country swing dancing.*

 QUESTIONS: *After your activity, go to a coffee shop or someplace quiet and talk about ways to maximize everyday moments. Have fun exploring ways you can foster intimacy with each other, even amid the chaos of everyday life.*

For example, in the morning, you might enjoy these activities:

- *Take a few moments to cuddle and affirm your love for each.*
- *Prepare breakfast together.*
- *Read a passage of Scripture and/or pray over the day together.*
- *Actually kiss good-bye before heading out the door!*

At midday, when you're typically apart, you might do the following:

- *Send quick texts or emails to say, "I love you and I'm thinking about you."*
- *Make phone calls to check in.*
- *Meet at a restaurant for a lunch date.*

In the evening, *you could reconnect in any of these ways:*

- *Greet your spouse with a kiss when he or she walks through the door.*
- *Make dinner together.*
- *Get the kids ready for bed together.*
- *Enjoy some downtime together.*
- *Pray together.*
- *Before rolling over and going to sleep, be sure to kiss good night—like you mean it!*

27 TOUCH

Hands, touchin' hands; reachin' out,
touchin' me, touchin' you.
—Neil Diamond, "Sweet Caroline"

MEANINGFUL TOUCH FOR COUPLES TAKES many forms. It may be the way a husband puts his hand on the small of his wife's back as they navigate a crowded room together, or the way a wife places her hand on her husband's knee as they're driving around town. Holding hands while walking, putting an arm around your mate's shoulders while sitting in the pew in church, cradling your beloved's face in your hands while you kiss, patting your spouse on the back in an effort to encourage him or her—all of these expressions communicate love, intimacy, and acceptance.

Studies show that people who are comfortable with touch in relationships are more "talkative" and "cheerful," while those uncomfortable with touching tend to be more "emotionally unstable and socially withdrawn."[1] It's also worth noting that physical touch is one of the five "love languages" identified by Dr. Gary Chapman as ways to express love emotionally. If physical touch is your spouse's primary love language, then it's especially important that you become an expert in expressing love in this way!

ACTIVITY: *Pick a typical activity, or get creative and come up with something that involves the sense of touch. Take a nature hike and experience the contrast in texture between tree bark, flower petals, and cold, hard stones (just avoid the poison ivy!). Or visit a fabric store and consider the differences between wool, silk, and other fabrics.*

QUESTIONS: *After your activity, go someplace quiet for coffee and dessert and discuss how the art of touch can communicate intimacy in your marriage. Is meaningful touch your primary love language? How do you feel when I put my arm around you in church or reach out for your hand when we're walking? What kind of touch do you respond to? What are some other ways we can incorporate meaningful touch into our daily routine?*

28 SIMPLE GIFTS

....

*A wise lover values not so much
the gift of Him Who loves as the
love of Him Who gives.*
—Thomas à Kempis, *The Imitation of Christ*

GIVING GIFTS TO YOUR SPOUSE can be a fun way to
build intimacy—if they're given in the right spirit
and for the right reasons! They're a simple way to
let your spouse know you value and appreciate him
or her. The gift doesn't have to be extravagant or
expensive. It could even be homemade. The important thing is that it conveys a meaningful message
about your feelings for your spouse or communi-
cates something particular about your relationship.

Have you ever mentioned needing a new pair of
winter gloves or a new golf putter only to have your
spouse surprise you a couple of days later with the
new item? The gloves might end up being too big
or the wrong color, and the putter might not match
the rest of your golf clubs. But at that point it
doesn't matter. The message that has been conveyed
is that your spouse listens to you and cares about
the things you care about. What do you usually say
when you receive a gift like this? "It's the thought
that counts." And that's absolutely true.

ACTIVITY: *Go shopping, preferably at the mall or a large department store. Then split up! Each of you should try to purchase something your spouse would find meaningful; something that reminds you of him or her. Again, don't feel the need to spend a lot of money. The item could be something as simple as a new neon cell-phone case for your wife to replace the one that broke, or a new ball cap featuring the logo of your husband's favorite team. After you've had a chance to find a gift, meet up again at a predetermined time for a gift exchange.*

Alternatively, if you have time in the days leading up to your date, why not try to make a gift for your spouse? It doesn't need to be complicated—perhaps putting together a simple scrapbook page of photos of the two of you having fun together, or even creating a playlist of some of your spouse's favorite songs and putting them on his or her iPod.

 QUESTIONS: *After you've exchanged gifts, discuss the following Questions: Why did you pick this gift? What about it made you think of me? How important are simple gifts like this to you in terms of communicating intimacy? Do you have any favorite gifts or mementos from early in our marriage that you still cherish?*

29 DOUBLE-DATE!

. . . .

Friendship is not a reward for our discrimination
and good taste in finding one another out.
It is the instrument by which God reveals
to each the beauties of all the others.
—C. S. Lewis, *The Four Loves*

IN GENERAL WE RECOMMEND THAT your dates be
devoted to couple time (i.e., uninterrupted time between just the two of you, without the distractions
of kids or other adults). *However*, once in a while,
it's a good idea to venture outside of that format and
enjoy a date with another couple.

For the purposes of this discussion, we'll assume
that you'll be dating with a "peer" couple—a couple
who is in generally the same stage of life you're in
and who is roughly the same age.

Just as on your regular dates, avoid the temptation to administrate during your double date.
For most couples during the childrearing years, the
standard procedure is to go out together and tell
story after story about the *kids*. They spend a great
deal of time and energy finding childcare so the
kids can stay at home, and then on their date, the
kids dominate the conversation! There's nothing
inherently wrong with this, of course. But if you
get to the end of the night and realize you know

everything there is to know about the other couple's *children* but very little about the *couple*, you've probably spent too much time on the joys and challenges of childrearing.

 ACTIVITY: *The rules for a double date are similar to those for your regular dates: (1) do something fun, and (2) if possible, experience something none of you have tried before. Just as you and your spouse build intimacy through these types of activities, you can also, as a couple, build stronger, deeper friendships by experiencing them with other couples. So go out and try some exotic food. Play laser tag or go swing dancing. Be creative and stretch your boundaries!*

QUESTIONS: *Ask questions and tell stories that will give you greater insights into the lives of your friends. For example, tell them your story, and let them tell you theirs. Even if you've known the other couple for years, you might not know some of the finer details of their dating, their wedding, and so on.*

If you share the same beliefs, don't be afraid to broach spiritual matters. What have you been learning in church lately? What have you been studying in a small group? Individually? As a couple?

---

30 CONNECT

*Communication's never been as
easy as today, and it would make
me happy when you've gone so
far away, if you'd send me an
e-mail that says "I love you."*
—Pet Shop Boys, "E-mail"

EARLIER WE TALKED ABOUT THE importance of maximizing everyday moments—of creating opportunities to build intimacy not only during dates but also amid the hustle and bustle of everyday life. We divided a typical day into three sections (when you're together in the early morning, when you're apart at midday, and when you're back together in the evening). This date is designed to help you hone your communication skills.

Technology has made it easier than ever before for husbands and wives to stay connected throughout the day. Smartphones, iPads, free wi-fi at restaurants, Skype, texting, email—in most cases you'd have to work really hard to find yourself in a situation that would prohibit you from sending a brief "I love you" to your spouse either in real time or in the form of a message he or she can read later.

ACTIVITY: *Have a high-tech treasure hunt in which the "treasure" you're looking for is . . . each other! Go somewhere you can use your electronic devices to full advantage, preferably a shopping center with free wi-fi. Then split up. After twenty minutes or so, contact each other through texts or phone calls. Leave clues as to your whereabouts (e.g., "I'm standing in a store with a bright-blue logo," or "I can see the main entrance from where I'm standing"). Can your partner figure out where you're at? If you're really adventurous and have a capable device, use Skype or FaceTime to communicate visually. Can your partner figure out where you're at by spotting clues that might be visible over your shoulder? Have fun using your electronic devices to track each other down. Once you've found your prize (i.e., each other), celebrate by going somewhere fun for dessert.*

 QUESTIONS: *After your activity, discuss some ways you can stay better connected during the hours you're apart throughout the week. Here are some ideas for staying connected:*

- *Send an occasional email or text to say, "I love you and I'm thinking about you."*
- *Write a nice message on your spouse's Facebook page.*
- *Call on your way home from work and ask, "Is there anything I can pick up for you at the store?"*
- *Call your spouse during a time you know he or she won't be able to answer the phone, and leave a romantic voice mail.*

- *Use Skype or FaceTime to say hi to each other visually.*
- *Meet for lunch.*
- *When practical to do so, drop by your spouse's office with a special treat (e.g., a cup of coffee or a snack) and say hi to colleagues and coworkers.*
- *Email or text a quick snapshot of what you're doing right now . . . even if it's just sitting at your desk at work or cutting vegetables at home.*

31 WE'RE THE BEST OF FRIENDS

This is my lover, this [is] my friend.
—Song of Songs 5:16

ARE YOU AND YOUR SPOUSE *friends*? In an article for Focus on the Family, Alyson Weasley suggests that friendship is among the most important components of marriage and summarizes twelve ways that couples can cultivate it:

1. Recognize that friendship building takes a lot of work—and time. Cut the fat out of your day.
2. Establish a time each week to spend quality time together—then guard that time with your lives!
3. Choose to spend time together rather than apart. This may mean sacrificing good things for a season, such as small groups, ministry, or bonding time with guys or gals.
4. Explore the interests of your spouse, be it baseball, art, musical theater, gardening, or hunting. Find out what they are passionate about and then join them. Often this takes a bit of sacrifice.
5. Take time to find common interests and then engage in them.

DATE 31

6. Use conflict to sharpen and purify friendship.
7. Nourish and care for one another. Be gentle with one another.
8. Accountability and mutual respect, including in the areas of sexuality, finances, and relationships, should be priorities.
9. Establish daily habits, especially praying together.
10. Affirm one another every day. Be intentional in communicating the other's strengths.
11. Be transparent with one another.
12. Communicate. Most experts agree that regular communication builds a friendship that weathers the storms of life.[1]

Did you notice anything about that list? That's right! You've been putting many of those principles into practice already through regular dating.

ACTIVITY: *Pick an activity that reinforces one of the concepts from Alyson Weasley's list. If you've already taken part in the "Shared Interests" date from earlier in the book, perhaps you could engage in the same shared activity again. Or choose another activity you both enjoy. Have fun!*

QUESTIONS: *After your activity, talk about what friendship means to you in the context of your marriage. Whom did you consider your best friend as a child? In what ways is having a same-sex best friend similar to having me as your best friend? In what ways is it different? What qualities do you see as essential in a friend? How can we work to forge stronger bonds of friendship in our marriage?*

3 2 DREAM MAKER

A dream you dream alone may be a dream, but a
dream two people dream together is a reality.
—Yoko Ono, *Grapefruit: A Book*
of Instructions and Drawings

DO YOU STILL HAVE DREAMS—goals in life that you'd
like to achieve? For many people, dreams are the
stuff of youth. By the time they get married and
start raising kids, they feel they need to set those
dreams aside in the interest of family.

Certainly, having a healthy family should be
among your top priorities. And there's no denying
that some things need to be set aside when one makes
the transition from single to married life. At the same
time, there's no reason to completely abandon your
dreams when you get married, so long as those desires
don't interfere with your pursuit of God or harm your
relationships with those you love. Neither should
having dreams and aspirations be the business only of
young people. Consider the following:[1]

- Andrea Bocelli didn't start singing opera
  until he was thirty-four. Some "experts" told
  him it was too late to begin an opera career.
- Famous chef Julia Child didn't learn to cook
  until she was almost forty and didn't launch
  her popular TV show until she was fifty.

- Laura Ingalls Wilder began writing as a columnist in her forties, and her popular Little House books were written and published when she was in her sixties!

The bottom line is that you're never too old to pursue a dream—and the pursuit of that dream doesn't necessarily have to upset the balance of your precious family. It's something for you and your spouse to think about together.

 ACTIVITY: *One of the basic tenets of this book is that you should try new and exciting things on your dates. But think a little harder about it this time. Is there something that either of you has always wanted to try? If it's doable within the context of a few hours allotted for your date, go for it! Or maybe your dream is bigger . . . something that can't be accomplished during a date. That's okay too. Just pick a fun activity and then discuss the logistics of your big dream later.*

 QUESTIONS: *After your activity, go someplace quiet and discuss your dreams and aspirations. Explore these Questions: Are there things you set aside when we got married that you'd like to consider pursuing? Is it wise to pursue them now? Is it possible? If so, how can I support you in achieving those dreams?*

---

33 MINDING YOUR "PLEASE" AND "THANK-YOUS"

....

Manners are a sensitive awareness of the feelings
of others. If you have that awareness, you have
good manners, no matter what fork you use.
—Emily Post

SADLY, IN MANY MARRIAGES THE basic principles of mannered behavior fly out the window. By the time you've been married to someone for five years, you've pretty much seen it all. You've watched your spouse throw up. You hear him or her snore—loudly—every night. Plus, you might be partners in parenthood now, and everyone knows there isn't time for silly things like holding the door and putting your napkin in your lap when you're busy wrangling children, right?

Wrong! It isn't always easy, but there's no reason why you can't practice reasonably good manners with your spouse even during the sometimes rough childrearing years. If your next-door neighbor comes over to borrow a hammer, you have no problem speaking politely to him. Why can't you do the same with your wife? If you have friends over for dinner, you dab the corners of your mouth and say, "Please pass the salt." Why can't you facilitate the same level of decorum when it's just you and the family around the table?

Emily Post's quote says it all. By practicing good manners, you're sending a message to your spouse (and other loved ones) that says, "I care about your feelings."

ACTIVITY: *If your budget allows, go somewhere fancy for dinner—a place where good manners are expected. Or try the ballet, opera, or another venue where a certain decorum is expected. Act the way you did when you were first dating. Impress your spouse with your thoughtfulness and consideration!*

QUESTIONS: *Either over dinner or after your activity, discuss the following Questions: When a man holds the door for a woman, is that courteous or sexist? Was your family big on manners and decorum? How did that make you feel? How can we encourage good manners in our home without obsessing about it or majoring in the minors? How important are manners amid the craziness of everyday life? What are some other things I can do to show you that I care about your feelings?*

---

3 4   REMEMBERING
AGAIN . . .

....

I can see you, your brown skin shining
in the sun. You got your hair combed
back and your sunglasses on, baby.
—Don Henley, "The Boys of Summer"

WE'VE TALKED AT LENGTH ABOUT the importance of
making *reminiscing* a prominent feature of your
dates. Remembering special times together can help
reawaken feelings of young love and can also help
you look forward to future good times as a couple.
Opening the floodgates of your shared memories
enables you to laugh together, cry together, and feel
more intimate.

A few years back a music group that was popular
during the eighties, when Erin and I (Greg) were in
high school, came to Colorado Springs. I thought
this would make a great date-night surprise, so I
bought tickets. We had a wonderful dinner at a
restaurant we'd never been to before. Later we found
ourselves in the concert hall, snuggling and reminiscing about our high school days.

For this date, you're going to spend more time
reminiscing, but with a more specific focus. You're
going to *recreate* a favorite date from before your
marriage!

ACTIVITY: *Talk about some of your favorite dates from your courtship period, and then pick one to recreate together. Do you still have any of the clothes you wore on your date (assuming you can still fit in them)? Even if you can't remember the exact clothes, perhaps you could get a little crazy by taking a trip to Goodwill in advance of your date and finding some now-out-of-style clothes from the eighties, nineties, or beyond, or whenever your dating glory days occurred. Are any nearby restaurants similar to the one you visited on your favorite date?*

 QUESTIONS: *After your activity, go someplace quiet to debrief and discuss the following Questions: Do you think we were successful in re-creating our chosen date? How did it make you feel? Do we have differing recollections about the details of our original date? In addition to the date we just recreated, what are some of your other favorite dating memories from before we married?*

35 ACCENTUATING
THE POSITIVE

....

I could list a million things I
love to like about you.
—"I Love the Way You Love Me," performed
by John Michael Montgomery

ALTHOUGH THIS BOOK IS ABOUT the benefits of marital dating, we've repeatedly stressed that *every day* presents you with the opportunity to connect with your spouse and pursue intimacy. Having couple time alone is important, but it's equally critical to maximize those everyday moments to bless your spouse and invest in your relationship.

Hopefully there are little things, simple things, you do for each other on a regular basis that communicate your love. It might be taking a few minutes away from the iPad and the TV to just sit and talk with your spouse about the day's events. Or perhaps you help with getting the kids bathed and in bed so your spouse can have a little downtime. Maybe you put the occasional "I love you" note in your spouse's lunch box.

The purpose of this date is simple. Think about the little things your spouse does every day that communicate love to you. Make a list of those things and then share it with your spouse.

ACTIVITY: *Prior to the date, compile your list. It doesn't have to be extensive. List just two or three things your spouse does that you appreciate and that make you feel loved. Then engage in a fun date-night activity. Go out for a nice dinner. Spend some time perusing the racks at your favorite bookshop. Take a relaxing walk around the park.*

 QUESTIONS: *After your activity, go someplace quiet and exchange the lists you made. Discuss the following Questions: Were you surprised by any of the things on my list? Why or why not? What are some other little things I can do to bless you and make you feel loved?*

36 THE LEARNING CURVE

It's what you learn after you know it all that counts.
—John Wooden, *Wooden on Leadership*

IF YOU THINK BACK TO your school days (whether elementary, high school, or college), you know the benefits of learning in a group setting. Perhaps you had a favorite study group or study partner to help you grasp certain concepts and ideas. When it came time for that algebra test, you were on your own. But you didn't get to that point on your own.

After graduation, many people assume that the time of learning—at least in a formal setting—has ended. But that need not be the case. Just as there is always something more to learn about your spouse, there's always something more to learn about the world outside your door. If God has gifted you with a natural affinity for science, mathematics, or the arts, it would be a shame for you to put those gifts on the shelf simply because you're no longer a full-time student.

Because learning is a communal process, is there a specific subject you and your spouse are both interested in that you could study together? Learning a new skill or expanding your knowledge of a specific subject is another great way for you to build intimacy!

ACTIVITY: *Take a class, attend a seminar, read an educational book, or visit a museum together. Find a subject that interests you both and expand your knowledge as a couple. Here are some possibilities:*

- *Take a pottery or woodworking class together.*
- *Attend a community lecture series.*
- *In the days leading up to your date, read a book on a subject that interests you and then discuss it on your date night.*
- *Visit a museum and explore an area of science or history that interests you.*
- *Watch a documentary and then discuss it afterward.*
- *Go stargazing together. Download an astronomy app for your phone that will help you identify constellations and other celestial bodies.*

 QUESTIONS: *After your activity, discuss your experience together, asking the following Questions: What did you learn during the course of our date? How can we continue to work together to expand our knowledge of our chosen subject? Are there other subjects we can explore together as a couple? How can we make learning fun?*

37 SOMETHING NEW

*A mind that is stretched by a new experience
can never go back to its old dimensions.*
—Oliver Wendell Holmes

ONE OF THE BASIC TENETS of marital dating is to find new and exciting experiences for you to enjoy together as a couple. Trying new activities, rather than simply repeating the same old things date after date, is a great way to recreate those feelings of excitement and discovery you experienced when you were first dating and getting to know each other.

While we've encouraged you to try new things throughout this book, make that your top priority for this date. Try something that you may not have even considered before. Get creative. Stretch your boundaries. Step outside your comfort zone. Don't be afraid to embrace something that lies far outside the realm of what you'd normally consider a dating activity. Enjoy the thrill of making a new discovery together!

 ACTIVITY: *Try something truly new to both of you. Go back through some of the suggested dates earlier in this book and pick a new activity or consider some of these suggestions:*

• *Go on a hot-air balloon ride.*

- *Go on a scavenger hunt. Pick a location and take your smartphones. Create a list of items and start taking pictures. The first person to capture a photo of every item on the list wins!*
- *Try indoor rock climbing.*
- *Rent Segways (you know, those sci-fi looking, two-wheeled cycles—www.segway.com) and tour the neighborhood, a park, and other locations.*

 QUESTIONS: *After your activity, discuss the following questions. As a child, were you afraid to try new things? Why or why not? How did it feel for you to step out of your comfort zone for our date? Is our chosen activity something we'd like to repeat in the future? What are some ways we can keep a spirit of discovery and adventure in our marriage? How can we avoid getting stuck in a rut?*

38 GRACE GIVEN, GRACE RECEIVED

....

What once was hurt, what once was friction;
what left a mark no longer stings, because
Grace makes beauty out of ugly things.
—U2, "Grace"

OFTEN IT SEEMS HARDEST TO give and receive grace
within our own families. It's easier to be forbearing
and forgiving toward strangers and acquaintances
than it is to demonstrate grace toward those who
live under the same roof with us. In many ways,
familiarity really does breed contempt!

Dr. Harold L. Arnold Jr., the founder of Discov-
ering Family International, has developed a unique
acrostic that helps married couples extend grace to
each other. Here's how it breaks down:

Give your spouse the benefit of the doubt.

Risk being honest [with yourself and with your
spouse].

Accept your spouse's feelings at face value.

Complain without criticizing [don't belittle your
spouse].

Embrace your differences.[1]

That's a great picture of G-R-A-C-E in marriage!
But since we've already established that your date
nights aren't for administrating your relationship or

for hashing out controversial or contentious issues, how might you incorporate G-R-A-C-E into your precious few hours of couple time? The answer is that you can accentuate the positive—talk about the ways your spouse is already excelling in extending grace in your relationship. This doesn't mean that your spouse is perfect or that there aren't areas you both need to work on. Extending grace simply means encouraging each other, lifting one another up, and agreeing to talk about the areas that need work at a later time.

 ACTIVITY: Feel free to engage in a typical date-night activity, so long as it's fun and exciting. If you want to do something more in line with the grace theme, consider finding a book on the Christian concept of grace and reading it in the days leading up to your date. Then discuss it during your time together. We'd recommend Philip Yancey's What's So Amazing about Grace? *as a good resource.[2]*

 QUESTIONS: After your activity, find a quiet coffee shop or another relaxing venue to discuss the following Questions: How would you define grace? Why is it so important? How can we extend grace to each other? To our children? To our extended family? In other relationships? Remember to keep your responses uplifting, positive, and encouraging.

39 COOKING UP SOMETHING FUN

Some people like to paint pictures, or do
gardening, or build a boat in the basement.
Other people get a tremendous pleasure
out of the kitchen, because cooking is just
as creative and imaginative an activity as
drawing, or wood carving, or music.
—Julia Child, in Lynn Gilbert's *Particular Passions*

HERE'S ANOTHER CHANCE FOR A stay-at-home date.
Earlier in the chapter we outlined a home date that
involved ordering a take-out meal. This time you're
going to work together to make the meal.

To be honest, it's okay if the dish you select
looks a little bit intimidating on paper. The more
complex the better! Why? Because cooking an exotic
meal together reinforces several of the important
components of marital dating, including (1) working together as a team; (2) stepping outside of your
comfort zone and the routine, mundane activities
you're accustomed to; and (3) doing something new
and exciting.

As you work on your meal together, don't feel
pressure to create something worthy of *MasterChef*
or a show on the Food Network. It's okay if the
risotto is a tad squishy or the salad dressing isn't

quite tangy enough. The goal is to have *fun* working together and creating something beautiful.

 ACTIVITY: *Pick your new recipe—maybe something exotic or ethnic. If time allows, go to the store together and pick out the freshest ingredients beforehand. And remember that there are plenty of unique recipes built upon basic ingredients, too. There's no need to buy rare and exotic (i.e., expensive) ingredients to create a new recipe. Go online to find recipe ideas. If you're feeling especially insecure about creating a new dish together, YouTube contains hundreds of step-by-step cooking videos from both professional and amateur chefs. Watching some of these user-friendly clips can help give you the boost of confidence you need to create your own masterpiece!*

 QUESTIONS: *While enjoying your meal together, discuss the following Questions: Do you like this recipe? Are there some other recipes we could try together? How do you feel we performed as a team on this project? Would this experience have been different if one person cooked the meal alone, as opposed to our working on it together? Did you learn anything about me during this process of making a meal together?*

> *She has her griefs and care, but the soft words, they*
> *are spoke so gentle, it makes it easier, easier to bear.*
> —"Try a Little Tenderness,"
> performed by Otis Redding

THINK ABOUT YOUR TYPICAL WEEKDAY. It's likely full of
challenges and frustrations, from rush-hour traffic
to obnoxious coworkers to meetings with the school
principal for an unruly child to car trouble, and on
and on. The hours during the day when you're apart
can be devastating to your self-esteem, your attitude,
and your faith in humanity. It's a tough world out
there.

On those especially trying days, how do you
treat your spouse when the family finally arrives
back together under the same roof? Are you snarky?
Do you take the cares and frustrations of the day out
on your spouse and kids? Is venting about your own
day more important to you than empathizing with
your spouse about his or her day?

The book of Proverbs reminds us that "a gentle
answer turns away wrath, but a harsh word stirs up
anger" (15:1). This is a crucial principle for husbands and wives who have hurried, harried lives (in
other words, *every* husband and wife). After a stress-
filled day, your time together should be filled with

tenderness. Your home should be a place of *refuge* from the trials and challenges of life—not a place to magnify and amplify them. Adopting this approach will help you share each other's burdens. This is one of the reasons why Scripture encourages us to "carry each other's burdens, and in this way you will fulfill the law of Christ" (Galatians 6:2) and admonishes us to "be quick to listen, slow to speak and slow to become angry" (James 1:19).

 ACTIVITY: *As usual, try something new and exciting. Whatever your activity, make sure to listen to your spouse and empathize with him or her. You might want to consider a quieter activity, without a lot of distractions and stimulation, that affords you the opportunity to zero in and focus on one another. Convey tenderness toward your mate throughout the evening.*

 QUESTIONS: *Either during your activity or in a quiet location afterward, discuss the following Questions: What things do I do that communicate tenderness toward you? Are there other ways I can communicate tenderness on a regular basis? Were your parents tender toward each other? How? Especially after long, tough days, how can we make a concerted effort to reconnect and show tenderness and empathy?*

---

41 COMMUNITY-MINDED

How far that little candle throws
his beams! So shines a good
deed in a naughty world.
—Portia, in William Shakespeare's
The Merchant of Venice

UP TO THIS POINT, THE majority of dates outlined
in this book have been introspective, focused on
fostering intimacy between you and your spouse,
to help you "turn toward" each other (see chapter
2). That will always be an important part of your
marriage. However, all of us, whether married or
single, can sometimes carry this concept too far. We
can become so focused on bettering ourselves, our
marriages, and our children that we become self-ab-
sorbed. We get so busy navel-gazing that we fail to
see the world around us.

That's why it's important for couples—especially
Christian couples—to look for opportunities to
serve others together. There's something beautiful
about husbands and wives working together to
invest time and energy in loving and serving others.
Some have described this as a "missional marriage."

The blessings of reaching out to others as a
husband-wife team are numerous. Susan Mathis
wrote,

DATE 41

Participating together in ministry opportunities can also help you to grow in your faith as a couple. Working side-by-side to fulfill the Great Commission—in whatever capacity—deepens your spiritual intimacy like little else can. . . Whenever you serve others, you become the hands and feet of your Savior.[1]

We couldn't have said it better ourselves! For this date, you're going to experience the joy and satisfaction of reaching out to someone in your neighborhood, church, or community.

 ACTIVITY: *Do a good deed for someone else! Look for opportunities to serve in your community. Here are a few ideas:*

- *Volunteer at a local soup kitchen or homeless shelter.*
- *Host a coat drive or clothing drive at your church.*
- *Help rake leaves, shovel snow, or otherwise beautify a neighbor's yard.*
- *Volunteer at your local library to help underprivileged kids learn to read or to help non-English speakers learn English.*

Need more ideas? Here are some additional activities— some can be incorporated into a date night, and some involve a longer-term commitment—by Samantha Krieger at StartMarriageRight.com:

1. Engage your server. *When you're out on a dinner date, let your server be a part of your relationship. Get to know him or her by asking questions. Find out if your server has any needs, and if you feel led, pray for him or her and share the gospel. Don't forget to leave a good tip!*

2. Prepare and deliver a meal. *Be watchful of who might be going through a crisis or simply struggling. Double up on a recipe one evening and give the other half away. Rally up your friends to contribute by creating a Care Calendar for the person/family in need.*

3. Consider becoming a foster couple or adopting. *Invest in the life of a child who desperately needs a loving home.*

4. Carry extra change. *When you're going shopping, keep extra change in your pockets with the intention of giving it away. Chances are you will run into a homeless person who can use it more than you.*

5. Start a playgroup. *Our community group started a playgroup that consisted of all the moms. We would meet randomly at local places like Chick-fil-A, the park, or the mall. We would get together and meet every other week at a different house. It was a great way to reach out and encourage fellow moms.*

6. Create an interest group or club. *What are you passionate about? Photography, running, football, quilting, going green? Invite a few people who love what you do, and do that thing together! You'll have a blast doing what you love and reaching out.*[2]

QUESTIONS: *After your service activity, go someplace quiet to unwind and discuss the following Questions: How do you feel about the service project we just completed together? Was your own family involved in community service? If so, was it considered an obligation or a privilege? How can we make acts of love and service a regular part of our marriage and family life rather than just isolated, one-time events?*

42 TRUST

You can trust us to stick with you through thick and
thin—to the bitter end. And you can trust us to keep
any secret of yours—closer than you keep it yourself.
But you cannot trust us to let you face trouble alone,
and go off without a word. We are your friends, Frodo.
—Merry to Frodo in J. R. R. Tolkien's
The Fellowship of the Ring

A FEW YEARS AGO, DURING a date at our favorite restaurant, Erin began sharing about how exhausted she gets while dealing with our children all day (our oldest is now in college). "Sometimes during the day, I feel like I'm losing my mind!" she said at one point. We laughed about how chaotic parenting can be at times, and we even referred to her as "Crazy Mama."

However, on the way home, we ended up having an argument about a sensitive topic (yeah, we obviously didn't follow our own advice). During the argument, I (Greg) made a rather ill-advised comment, suggesting that the argument was Erin's fault because she wasn't thinking clearly. "Remember dinner?" I said. "You've already admitted that you're losing your mind!"

Not only was the comment not funny; it actually weakened our relationship. Why? Because

I used something against Erin that she'd shared during an intimate conversation. Nobody wants to reveal private and sacred information when it might later be used against them! When couples feel unsafe sharing their emotions, their hearts tend to close, and they disconnect emotionally from each other. On the other hand, when people feel safe, they are naturally inclined to open their hearts and spirits, and intimacy occurs effortlessly and naturally.

 ACTIVITY: *There are many levels of trust within marriage—emotional, relational, spiritual, physical, and so on. Consider a fun activity that reinforces the concept of trust between you and your spouse. It could be anything from a ropes course to skydiving to singing karaoke or scaling a climbing wall. Like the teamwork date, it should be an activity that requires you to rely on each other in order to complete—something that requires you to say to one another, "I've got your back."*

 QUESTIONS: *After your activity, explore the following Questions: Did you trust me during our chosen activity? Would you have done the same thing with someone else? With a stranger? How can we ensure that our marriage is always a safe environment to share private and sensitive information?*

43 HOME DATE!

*Home, where my thought's escaping,
home, where my music's playing, home,
where my love lies waiting . . .*
—Simon and Garfunkel,
"Homeward Bound"

WE'VE ALREADY HIGHLIGHTED SOME DATES that lend themselves to staying at home. However, this is a concept that warrants revisiting. For one thing, we know that even in the best of economic times, going out on a regular basis can become an expensive proposition for many couples. Staying at home and spending quality time together after the kids are in bed can be a cost-effective way for couples to build intimacy and "turn toward" each other. For another thing, your home is also, in many ways, the center-piece of your married and family life. Such a setting lends itself to fostering connection and intimacy.

Oh, and one more thing. A home date can also serve as a great plan B when your childcare falls through, which will inevitably happen more often than you'd like. A last-minute change of plans doesn't automatically mean that your date night has to be canceled. Sometimes, even when it comes to an unexpected change to your date-night plans, "there's no place like home."

ACTIVITY: *Just because you're staying home doesn't mean you have to dress like a slob. Get out of those sweatpants and put a little effort into looking nice for your spouse. As for actual activities, use your imagination. For example, once the kids are asleep, go out on your back porch, grill some steaks, and enjoy a gourmet meal under the stars. If it's cold outside, put a tablecloth down in front of the fireplace and enjoy your meal there.*

QUESTIONS: *If your chosen activity doesn't allow it, make sure you reserve some time afterward to connect through good conversation. Catch up on the events of the day and the week. Ask yourselves, "Are there other ways we can foster intimacy in our relationship on a regular basis when we're at home?"*

44 FAMILY DATE

Rejoice with your family in the beautiful land of life!
—Albert Einstein, letter to Paul Ehrenfest, June 1918

ONCE AGAIN, IT'S TIME TO break from the traditional marital-dating template. Instead of enjoying quiet, uninterrupted couple time, you're going to involve the entire family! This isn't something you should do frequently, but there are certainly benefits to the occasional family outing of this nature.

A family date sets a great example for your kids. It allows you to be affectionate and romantic with each other in their presence. We're not talking about "making out" in front of them—gross! However, it's entirely appropriate for husbands and wives to show affection for each other in front of their kids. It demonstrates a healthy male-female dynamic and sends the message that married life can be *fun*—it's not just drudgery and arguing over bills.

Dr. Ken R. Canfield, founder of the National Center for Fathering, explains how marital dating can make a dramatic impact on your children:

> Your son is taking subconscious notes. He's asking, "How should I treat women?" "What does it mean to be a husband?" Your daughter also has her eye on you. The thought of giving

herself to a man in marriage can be frightening. She's asking herself how well her mother fared in the deal. Your children watch when you open car doors for your wife. They listen closely when you compliment her on how radiant she looks in that new dress, or express your appreciation for all she does for you.[1]

 ACTIVITY: *Choose a Saturday or another time when both you and the kids are free, and engage in something fun. Don't be afraid to call it a "family date." Many of the same principles apply. It's a chance to get away, invest in one another, and form deeper bonds. Go to a new restaurant, drive to a neighboring town to see the sights, play miniature golf or disc golf, take a picnic to the park, go sightseeing at some local landmarks, and so on.*

 QUESTIONS: *After the date is over and it's just the two of you again—perhaps at night in bed—discuss the day's family date. Consider the following Questions: Did your parents go on dates when you were young? Did they model a healthy marriage for you? Can our own commitment to marital dating model healthy marriage concepts for our kids? What are some ways we can maximize everyday moments with our children in the same way we've endeavored to do so in our marriage?*

45 WITH THANKSGIVING

> *In everyone's life, at some time, our inner fire goes*
> *out. It is then burst into flame by an encounter with*
> *another human being. We should all be thankful*
> *for those people who rekindle the inner spirit.*
> —Albert Schweitzer

AT THANKSGIVING WE SET ASIDE time to reflect on the blessings God has given us—our families, our friends, our health, our jobs, our freedom. These are all tremendous gifts. But during significant events like the Thanksgiving holiday, we tend to look at the big picture—attempting to acknowledge *all* of the many blessings God has given us rather than narrowing in on specifics.

This is especially true when it comes to our spouses. It's one thing to say, "Thank You, God, for my wonderful wife," while everyone is sitting around the dinner table. That's a nice gesture, but let's be honest; it's not very specific, and besides, it's what everyone expects you to say. So it's important that you also take time alone with your spouse to tell him or her directly *why* you're thankful. This should involve not only thanking God but also thanking your partner—*directly* and *specifically*—for the things he or she does that bless and enrich your life. Throughout the year, we should make a concerted effort to express gratitude *for* our spouses and *to* our spouses!

ACTIVITY: *With Thanksgiving drawing near—and the frantic preparations it likely entails for you—use this opportunity to go someplace quiet and relaxing for dinner. Find a restaurant that doesn't have anything on the menu resembling turkey and dressing!*

QUESTIONS: *Either over dinner or in a quiet location afterward, take turns sharing specific reasons why you're thankful for your mate. Make a list if you feel it would be helpful. Here are some ways you might complete the sentence "I'm thankful for you because . . ."*

> *I have someone to laugh with.*
> *I have someone to hold me when life gets hard.*
> *I have someone to come home to.*
> *I have someone to challenge me.*
> *I have someone to cuddle with!*

Once you've made a list of general qualities, dig deeper. Talk about a specific time recently when your spouse made you laugh or otherwise cheered you up. If you're thankful for your spouse's parenting skills, cite a specific example of those skills in action. This process has the potential to be a time of great connection, reminiscing, and intimacy.

---

46 A CHRISTMAS DATE

. . . .

Christmas gift suggestions: To your enemy, forgiveness.
To an opponent, tolerance. To a friend, your heart.
To a customer, service. To all, charity. To every
child, a good example. To yourself, respect.
—Author unknown

WHAT BETTER WAY TO TAKE the focus off ourselves
and the "stuff" that somehow seems so important
at Christmas? The Bible reminds us that "the Son of
Man did not come to be served, *but to serve*, and to
give his life as a ransom for many" (Matthew 20:28).
The Child in the manger is a portrait not of kingly
elegance and excess but of humility and service.

This date will give you the opportunity to
take a break from the holiday grind and invest *as a*
couple in the well-being of someone else. Through
volunteering your time and talent in service to
others, you'll experience the satisfaction of making
a positive impact on an individual, a group, or even
your entire community. What's more, you'll likely
experience a deeper marital bond and sense of intimacy through serving together.

Your Christmas date can go one of two ways.
You might want to simply combine your date and
your service project into one event. Or if your
crowded holiday calendar allows, you can go on a

regular date to plan and talk about your volunteer ideas and then actually perform your act of service at a later time—perhaps on a Saturday. This second approach would allow you to enjoy some quality couple time on your date and then involve your kids in the actual service project later.

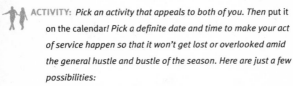

ACTIVITY: *Pick an activity that appeals to both of you. Then put it on the calendar! Pick a definite date and time to make your act of service happen so that it won't get lost or overlooked amid the general hustle and bustle of the season. Here are just a few possibilities:*

- *Go to a local store and inquire about the possibility of gift-wrapping shoppers' presents for a small donation. Then give the money to a local charity or an organization such as Compassion International or World Vision.*

- *Do you know someone who will be alone at Christmas? Perhaps there's a widower living nearby or a college student who can't afford to travel home for the holidays. Consider buying a present, baking Christmas cookies, or doing something else to let this person know that he or she is loved. You might even invite this person to take part in your family's own Christmas festivities.*

- *Gather some friends and family members and go Christmas caroling. Ask local nursing homes and care facilities about the possibility of spending an evening singing Christmas carols for the residents.*

- *Offer to help neighbors get their home ready for Christmas. Perhaps an older couple or a single-parent family near you could use assistance with shoveling snow, hanging Christmas lights, putting up decorations, or other tasks.*

QUESTIONS: *After your activity, go somewhere quiet for some coffee, hot chocolate, or an eggnog latte and discuss the following Questions: What was your all-time favorite Christmas gift? What's the worst Christmas gift you've ever received? What is one of your favorite Christmas memories?*

47 WHAT ARE YOU DOING NEW YEAR'S EVE?

We were strangers starting out on a journey,
never dreaming what we'd have to go
through. Now here we are, and I'm suddenly
standing at the beginning with you.
—"At the Beginning," performed by Richard Marx
and Donna Lewis in *Anastasia*

YOUR DATING JOURNEY HAS COME full circle! If you started with the "New Year's Date," you've enjoyed a full year of marital-dating bliss. At least we hope so! Whether you committed to dating once a week, once a month, or some other frequency, these date-night ideas have taken you on a journey designed to foster intimacy, connection, excitement, and yes, that word we keep repeating: *fun.*

As the year draws to a close, it's a great time to take stock of what you've learned over the preceding months. Did you set goals for your relationship at the beginning of the year? Did making regular date nights a priority help you achieve those goals? Make this New Year's Eve an opportunity to celebrate where you've been, what you've accomplished, and how you'd like to continue nurturing your relationship in the coming year.

Remember, dating your spouse should remain

a regular feature of your marriage for as long as you both shall live. As we've been saying, there's always something new to learn about your spouse, and engaging in fun date-night activities is a great way to discover those things!

ACTIVITY: *Go somewhere romantic for New Year's Eve. Have a candlelight dinner. Go dancing. Or if that seems too conventional for you, try something unexpected and different. Grab some fast food and drive up to your favorite romantic overlook. Even if the temperatures outside are frigid, we're sure you can figure out a way to stay warm!*

QUESTIONS: *If you've had quite a few date nights already, take some time to reflect on them and discuss the following Questions: Which dates were your favorites? Which ones didn't turn out the way you expected? Which ones would you like to to repeat? How can we continue to make dating a priority in our marriage over the months and years ahead? Finish your date night with prayer, committing your marriage to the Lord for the coming year.*

---

48 THE ANNIVERSARY OF YOUR FIRST DATE

*Dating is pressure and tension. What is a date,
really, but a job interview that lasts all night?*
—Jerry Seinfeld, comedian

PICTURE THE SCENE: A MARRIED couple is driving around town, simply running errands or heading home from the store. Suddenly the wife exclaims, "Honey! I just realized that twelve years ago, on this very night, we had our first date! Can you believe it? How time flies!" She puts her hand on her husband's knee and smiles wistfully.

Meanwhile, the husband, in a state of utter shock and confusion, can only blurt, "Uh, *of course* it's the twelfth anniversary of our first date! I was just going to mention that fact. Oh, what wonderful memories I have of that night. What did we do again?"

On the other hand, some of you may not even have had a distinct first-date experience. That's certainly true of us. Our relationship grew and flourished within the context of platonic friendship rather than through a formal dating scenario. In fact, our decision to start dating—to take our relationship to the next level—came on a cruise ship! Don't worry, there's nothing salacious to report. I

(Greg) was on the cruise with my mom and dad, and Erin was employed as a nanny for another couple on the ship. It was during the cruise that Erin and I articulated our feelings for each other and agreed to pursue a romantic relationship. Shades of *The Love Boat*!

In any event, assuming you did begin dating in more conventional terms, it might not be that important to you to trace your first date back to a specific day on the calendar. Whether you can pinpoint that actual anniversary of your first date or not, you can certainly take steps to *recreate* it. We discussed the idea of re-creating a date. That date involved reliving one of your *favorite* or most memorable dates. This date is a bit more specific. If your very first date truly wasn't that noteworthy or, in the case of some couples, was an unmitigated disaster, don't sweat it. Recreate it anyway and redeem the time!

ACTIVITY: *Whether you're reenacting your very first date or the date when you got engaged, you likely won't be able to recreate everything down to the last detail. You probably don't even live in the same city where you first met. And even if you do, the romantic restaurant where you had your first rendezvous may have long since closed its doors. Find a suitable alternative that evokes memories of that first date, even if some of the particulars are different. If you saw a movie, find the same film on DVD or online and watch it again at home. If you took pictures on your first date, find the photos and enjoy reliving those times (and laugh at how funny your clothes and hairstyles were).*

QUESTIONS: *This is a great opportunity to remember, to compare notes, and probably to laugh as well. After your activity, discuss the following Questions: Were you nervous before our first date? Do you remember any funny stories? Did anything go wrong on our date — something that seemed utterly cata-strophic at the time but that we laugh about now? Were your friends and family members enthusiastic about the prospect of our dating? After that first date, did you have any second thoughts about moving forward? At what point during our dating relationship did you know I was "the one"?*

4 9   W E D D I N G   A N N I V E R S A R Y

....

> *What greater thing is there for human souls, than*
> *to feel that they are joined for life . . . to be with*
> *each other in silent unspeakable memories.*
> —George Eliot, *Adam Bede*

AS DATES GO, THE ANNIVERSARY date is probably the biggest no-brainer in the history of no-brainers, with the other possible candidate being the Valentine's Day date. Even if you've had a terrible track record for dating since you got married, chances are you've gone out on at least one or two dates to celebrate your wedding anniversary.

A few hours of uninterrupted couple time is the perfect opportunity to reminisce, to celebrate, to thank God, and to commemorate an event that is among the most momentous occasions of your entire life.

ACTIVITY: *If you've celebrated your wedding anniversary with a romantic date in the past, don't feel pressured to deviate significantly from that formula now. There's nothing wrong with having a nice candlelight dinner to celebrate your years of wedded bliss. At the same time, if a romantic date is the norm for you on your anniversary, why not try something new this year? Go to a drive-through restaurant and then take your food to the park for a picnic. Try writing each other a love poem.*

Have T-shirts made commemorating your anniversary and then wear them to the zoo, the local amusement park, or another attraction. In addition, consider the following ideas:

- Get out your wedding photo album or wedding video and relive the memories from your special day.
- Work together on making a new video—with updated photos and clips from your years of marriage—to celebrate your journey together thus far.
- Do any of your groomsmen or bridesmaids still live within driving distance? If so, explore the double-date idea by inviting them and their spouses to join you at a restaurant in celebration of your anniversary. Have fun sharing memories together.
- Consider a night or weekend away to celebrate your anniversary in true uninterrupted style. This is a particularly good option for milestone anniversaries, such as your tenth, fifteenth, twenty-fifth, and so on.

 QUESTIONS: *Whether you engage in a full weekend away or a quick visit to a nearby diner, an anniversary date is all about reminiscing. Discuss the following Questions: Do you remember any funny stories from our wedding day? Were you stressed? Can you recall anything specific about the pastor's message aside from the standard exchange of vows? What are some of your favorite memories from our honeymoon? If we had the chance to do our wedding and honeymoon again, would we change anything?*

50 – 51 BIRTHDAY . . .
TIMES TWO!

A diplomat is a man who always remembers a
woman's birthday but never remembers her age.
—attributed to Robert Frost

BIRTHDAYS ARE A BIG DEAL when you're a kid. But
when you're an adult, birthdays are very different.
For one thing, the prospect of being one year older
isn't as exciting as it was when you were young. And
for another, grown-ups don't really feel the need to
make birthdays an event. At the most, your coworkers might put up a couple of birthday balloons in
your cubicle and wish you well. Or you might get
together for coffee with a friend. And that's it.

If there's anyone who's going to make a big deal
of your birthday as an adult—who will fawn over
you and make you feel as if you're the most important person in the universe—it should be your
spouse! Celebrating your mate's birthday and putting forth a little extra effort to make him or her feel
special are great ways to communicate affection and
admiration. We know of some spouses who even
take a vacation day from work to spend the day with
their husbands or wives on birthday occasions.

So go ahead, turn your mate's birthday—an
occasion many of us dread as we get older—into

an opportunity to make him or her feel special, affirmed, and loved!

ACTIVITY: *There are two approaches you might take when planning a birthday date. The first is to let the birthday girl or boy plan all of the activities. After all, it's your spouse's birthday— he or she should be able to choose what to do, right? Another option would be for you to plan the entire date and surprise the birthday boy or girl.*

As with any date, the operative word for a birthday date is fun. *Taking extra care to ensure that your spouse feels like a kid again can be a great way to convey your love for him or her.*

QUESTIONS: *After your activity, discuss the following questions: What are some of your favorite birthday memories from childhood? What makes them so special? What is your favorite birthday activity as an adult? Do you dread the idea of having birthdays and getting older? How can I help make sure that birthdays for you are uplifting and fulfilling?*

---

52 MILESTONES

....

To get the full value of joy you must
have someone to divide it with.
—Mark Twain

THE FINAL DATE IN OUR list of fifty-two could actually turn into *several* dates, depending on how many events or milestones you choose to commemorate in this way. Basically, this is a chance for you and your spouse to celebrate any number of significant events in your lives by setting aside some quality couple time together. Some dates happen "just because," and others are tied to certain life developments or special occasions. Either way, the goal is the same: to grow closer to your spouse, to have fun, and to invest in your relationship. There's *always* a good excuse to go on a date!

With that said, here are some life events that you might consider celebrating or commemorating with your spouse.

A Promotion at Work

ACTIVITY: *Go out for dinner someplace nice, especially if your promotion involved an increase in salary.*

QUESTIONS: *If you got the promotion, be sure to thank your spouse for supporting and encouraging you as a significant breadwinner in achieving this major milestone. If your spouse got the promotion, make an effort to highlight the skills and character traits that likely contributed to the recognition received at work.*

Completion of a Degree or Other Coursework

 ACTIVITY: *Whether your classes took place online or on campus, schedule your "graduation date" during the time that normally would have been occupied by your studies. This will drive home the fact that you're done with your classes, and that you now have a few extra hours in your week to pursue other activities . . . such as dating your spouse!*

 QUESTIONS: *Whether or not you talk specifically about your spouse's degree during your date will depend on your spouse. He or she may take pleasure and pride in sharing with you some of the nuggets of wisdom that were gained while earning the degree. On the other hand, after studying for finals and "firing on all cylinders" in that final push before graduation, the last thing some students want to do is talk about school! If that's the case for your spouse, make sure your date night is relaxing and fun—a welcome reprieve from talk about economics or theology or business or English.*

Achievement of a Personal Goal or Objective

ACTIVITY: *Perhaps your spouse had a goal of losing twenty pounds or completing a rigorous exercise program. Or maybe he or she has just completed another difficult project—writing a book, building a fence in the backyard, volunteering in a high-risk youth program, or painting the house. Take him or her out on the town to celebrate the achievement!*

QUESTIONS: *This is another chance to show a genuine interest in the things that matter to your spouse. Be sure to offer lots of praise and affirmation and to also ask Questions: How do you feel now that you've reached your goal? Would you ever commit to doing something like that again? Do you feel you've grown emotionally or spiritually as a result of completing your task?*

Completion of Chemotherapy or Another Intensive Medical Procedure

ACTIVITY: *Following a prolonged illness or another physical challenge, going out and feeling "normal" again might just be the thing to brighten your mate's spirits. Take your spouse to a nice restaurant or engage in a recreational activity of his or her choosing.*

QUESTIONS: *Although you didn't experience the actual physical symptoms, enduring a serious illness like cancer is certainly*

something that spouses do together. During your date, take time to debrief and talk about how the experience has changed both of you. If your spouse was the one who was ill, make sure to praise him or her for demonstrating strength and resilience in the face of difficult odds. And if you were sick, make every effort to let your spouse know how grateful you are to him or her for walking with you on this journey. End the evening by praying together and giving thanks to God for bringing you and your family through this difficult time. Ask Him to continue drawing you closer to each other and closer to Him through whatever lies ahead—the good and the bad—in your marriage.

Notes

Date 5

1. Gary Smalley and John Trent, *The Blessing* (New York: Simon & Schuster, 1986), chapters 3–5.
2. Ibid., 29.
3. Ibid., 30.
4. Ibid., 31.
5. Ibid., 32.
6. Gary Smalley and John Trent, *The Gift of the Blessing* (Nashville: Thomas Nelson, 2004).

Date 8

1. US Department of Transportation, Federal Highway Administration, *Summary of Travel Trends: 2009 National Household Travel Survey* (Washington, DC: US Department of Transportation, 2011), 30–32, 53, accessed April 9, 2013, http://nhts.ornl.gov/2009/pub/stt.pdf.

Date 9

1. Sari Harrar and Rita DeMaria, *The 7 Stages of Marriage* (Pleasantville, NY: Reader's Digest Books, 2007), cited in Random Facts, "63 Interesting Facts about . . . Marriage,"

http://facts.randomhistory.com/interesting
-facts-about-marriage.html.

2. Dictionary.com, s.v. "intimacy," accessed April
   11, 2013, http://dictionary.reference.com
   /browse/intimacy.

Date 10

1. *Merriam-Webster Online*, s.v. "cherish," accessed
   April 11, 2013, http://www.merriam-webster
   .com/dictionary/cherish.

Date 13

1. C. S. Lewis, *Out of the Silent Planet* (New York:
   Scribner, 1996), 74.

Date 14

1. Christie Nicholson, "The Humor Gap: Men and
   Women See Laughter Differently in Romance,"
   Scientific American, April 8, 2010, http://www
   .scientificamerican.com/article.cfm?id=the
   -humor-gap.

2. Ibid.

3. Study conducted by Michael Miller et. al., University of Maryland School of Medicine (2005),
   cited in University of Maryland Medical Center,
   "University of Maryland School of Medicine
   Study Shows Laughter Helps Blood Vessels

Function Better," March 7, 2005, http://www
.umm.edu/news/releases/laughter2.htm.

4. R. Morgan Griffin, "Give Your Body a Boost—
   with Laughter," "Health and Balance," WebMD,
   accessed April 10, 2013, http://www.webmd
   .com/balance/features/give-your-body-boost
   -with-laughter.

5. Ibid.

Date 16

1. Bureau of Labor Statistics, "American Time Use
   Survey," 2011, http://www.bls.gov/tus/charts
   /leisure.htm.

2. James H. O'Keefe et al., "Potential Adverse Car-
   diovascular Effects from Excessive Endurance
   Exercise," *Mayo Clinic Proceedings* 87, no. 6
   (June 2012), doi:10.1016/j.mayocp.2012
   .04.005, cited in news release, *Mayo Clinic Proceedings*, June 4, 2012, http://www.mayoclinic
   proceedings.org/webfiles/images/journals/jmcp
   /jmcp_pr87_6_2.pdf.

Date 20

1. WebMD, "The Effects of Stress on Your
   Body," July 23, 2012, accessed April 10, 2013,
   http://www.webmd.com/mental-health
   /effects-of-stress-on-your-body.

2. Study conducted by the University of Jyvaskyla, Finland, cited in "Stressed Parents Risk Having Burnt-Out Children, Study Finds," *Telegraph*, January 21, 2010, accessed April 10, 2013, http://www.telegraph.co.uk /health/healthnews/7040358/Stressed-parents -risk-having-burnt-out-children-study-finds .html.

3. Richard Swenson, *Margin: Restoring Emotional, Physical, Financial, and Time Reserves to Overloaded Lives* (Colorado Springs: NavPress, 2004), 69.

Date 27

1. Studies cited in Gary Smalley and John Trent, *The Gift of the Blessing* (Nashville: Thomas Nelson, 1993), 193.

Date 31

1. Adapted from Alyson Weasley, "Twelve Steps to a Deeper Friendship with Your Spouse," "Marriage and Relationships," Focusonthe Family.com, (2007), http://www.focusonthe family.com/marriage/sex_and_intimacy/the _role_of_friendship_in_marriage/ten_steps _to_a_deeper_friendship_with_your_spouse .aspx.

Date 32

1. Adapted from Kristen Houghton, "Dreams Have No Age Limit: Famous People Who Started Late," *The Blog*, Huffpost Healthy Living, April 6, 2010, accessed April 11, 2013, http://www.huffingtonpost.com /kristen-houghton/dreams-have-no-age-limit _b_525358.html.

Date 38

1. Harold L. Arnold Jr., "A Measure of Grace," "Marriage and Relationships," Focusonthe Family.com, 2008, http://www.focusonthefamily .com/marriage/marriage_challenges/marriage _in_the_melting_pot/a_measure_of_grace .aspx.

2. Philip Yancey, *What's So Amazing about Grace?* (Grand Rapids: Zondervan, 2002).

Date 41

1. Susan Mathis, "Serving Together as a Couple," "Marriage and Relationships," Focusonthe Family.com, 2011, http://www.focusonthefamily .com/marriage/daily_living/serving-together .aspx.

2. Adapted from Samantha Krieger, "Missional Marriage: 10 Practical Ways to Serve Other People," StartMarriageRight.com, December

2011, http://www.startmarriageright.com
/2011/12/missional-marriage-10-practical-ways
-to-serve-other-people/, used with permission.

Date 44

1. Ken R. Canfield, "What Children Gain When
   You Love Their Mother," Fathers.com, April 30,
   2007, accessed April 11, 2013, http://www
   .fathers.com/content/index.php?option=com
   _content&task=view&id=295&Itemid=63.